At Issue

Do Abstinence Programs Work?

Other Books in the At Issue Series:

At Issue

Do Abstinence Programs Work?

Christina Fisanick, Book Editor

GREENHAVEN PRESS

A part of Gale, Cengage Learning

GALE
CENGAGE Learning·

Detroit • New York • San Francisco • New Haven, Conn • Waterville, Maine • London

Christine Nasso, *Publisher*
Elizabeth Des Chenes, *Managing Editor*

© 2010 Greenhaven Press, a part of Gale, Cengage Learning.

Gale and Greenhaven Press are registered trademarks used herein under license.

For more information, contact:
Greenhaven Press
27500 Drake Rd.
Farmington Hills, MI 48331-3535
Or you can visit our Internet site at gale.cengage.com

For product information and technology assistance, contact us at

Gale Customer Support, 1-800-877-4253
For permission to use material from this text or product, submit all requests online at www.cengage.com/permissions

Further permissions questions can be emailed to permissionrequest@cengage.com

Articles in Greenhaven Press anthologies are often edited for length to meet page requirements. In addition, original titles of these works are changed to clearly present the main thesis and to explicitly indicate the author's opinion. Every effort is made to ensure that Greenhaven Press accurately reflects the original intent of the authors. Every effort has been made to trace the owners of copyrighted material.

Cover image © Images.com/Corbis.

LIBRARY OF CONGRESS CATALOGING-IN-PUBLICATION DATA

Do abstinence programs work? / Christina Fisanick, book editor.
    p. cm. -- (At issue)
Includes bibliographical references and index.
ISBN-13: 978-0-7377-4292-3 (hardcover)
ISBN-13: 978-0-7377-4291-6 (pbk.)
1. Youth--Sexual behavior--Juvenile literature. 2. Sexual abstinence--Juvenile literature. 3. Sex instruction for teenagers--Juvenile literature. I. Fisanick, Christina.
  HQ27.D69 2010
  306.73'208350973--dc22

                                  2009027201

Printed in the United States of America
2 3 4 5 6 7 13 12 11 10

Contents

Introduction

On World AIDS Day in 2008, the Gay, Lesbian and Straight Education Network (GLSEN) announced that abstinence-only education is a detriment to the health and well being of gay and lesbian students because most of the programs fail to educate them about safe sex practices. According to Dr. Eliza Byard, GLSEN's executive director, "We must commit ourselves as a nation to providing proper and comprehensive education to our youth about how they can reduce the chance of contracting HIV/AIDS." Other organizations have recently spoken out against abstinence-only education, arguing that it discriminates against gay and lesbian students because they cannot legally marry when they become adults. However, proponents of abstinence-only education believe that promoting abstinence until marriage is the only way to ensure the safety and well being of all young people who might consider engaging in premarital sex.

There is no doubt that the most effective way to prevent the spread of sexually transmitted diseases is through abstinence from sexual intercourse. However, given that abstinence-only programs teach that people should wait until marriage before engaging in sex, an obvious problem arises for gay and lesbian people who are not legally allowed to marry in nearly all states. The Sexuality Information and Education Council of the United States (SIECUS) notes that "Unlike their heterosexual peers who may someday marry, gay and lesbian teens are essentially told that their sexual feelings will always conflict with society's standards and that they should never engage in sexual activity." Therefore, opponents of abstinence-only sex education insist that teaching abstinence affords gay and lesbian teens little opportunity for understanding their own sexuality and learning about safe sex practices.

But proponents of abstinence-only education maintain that it remains the best method of educating teens about sex, especially young, gay men. Focus on the Family, a Christian organization dedicated to preserving the American family and to upholding conservative social values, asserts that "any sexual behavior among unmarried young people is risky, especially homosexual behavior." They cite a 2006 study published by the Centers for Disease Control and Prevention (CDC) which demonstrates that gay men are far more likely to contract syphilis, gonorrhea, and HIV than heterosexual men. Given this data, organizations like Focus on the Family insist that abstinence-only education is essential for the well being of society, especially those members most at risk—gay young men.

However, others contend that abstinence-only education pushes an agenda that makes gay and lesbian students feel alienated from their peers and unsafe in a setting where they should be most protected. The 2007 National School Climate Survey conducted by GLSEN indicates that gay and lesbian students in schools with abstinence-only curricula reported higher levels of bullying and even assault than gay and lesbian students in schools without abstinence-only curricula. Some critics have argued that these higher levels of harassment are the result of specific terminology and attitudes expressed in abstinence-only materials. According to a position statement by the American Civil Liberties Union (ACLU), "By talking only about sex within marriage and teaching about STDs [sexually transmitted diseases] as a form of moral punishment for homosexuality, abstinence-only-until-marriage programs not only undermine efforts to educate teens about protecting their health, but create a hostile learning environment for lesbian and gay students."

Nonetheless, supporters of abstinence-only sex education believe that this approach is not solely about protecting young people from pregnancy and sexually transmitted diseases; it is also about giving students crucial life skills. In April 2008, the

Heritage Foundation, a conservative think tank, studied fifteen abstinence-only programs across the United States and concluded that the approach is far more successful than detractors believe. In fact, the study shows that not only did these programs lower the rate at which young people were having sex outside of marriage, but also that they changed student perceptions about sex and sexuality. In a press release, the Foundation declared that teaching abstinence-only education "also provides youths with valuable life and decision-making skills that lay the foundation for personal responsibility and developing healthy relationships and marriages later in life." In other words, even if the curricula of most abstinence-only programs exclude information about gay and lesbian relationships, they are still capable of teaching all young people important lessons about making smart choices.

Soon after President Barack Obama took office in 2009, he radically cut funding to abstinence-only programs, arguing that they have been largely ineffective in reducing rates of teen pregnancy and sexually transmitted diseases. It is believed that much of the new budget for sex education will be allotted for comprehensive programs designed to teach both abstinence and safe sex practices. Concerns among gay and lesbian activists have not diminished, however. After all, there is no guarantee that comprehensive sex education will be any more supportive of gay and lesbian relationships than abstinence-only programs. In *At Issue: Do Abstinence Programs Work?* the authors present a variety of viewpoints on this divisive subject, including the role of parents in educating their children about sex, the impact of abstinence-only education on teen health, and whether comprehensive sex education is more effective than abstinence-only education. It is clear that all parties involved care about the well being of young people, but determining how best to teach them about sex and sexuality will continue to be a matter for intense debate.

1

Parents Should Educate Their Teens About Sex

Naomi Schaefer Riley

Naomi Schaefer Riley is the Taste editor for The Wall Street Journal.

Ignorance of the basic concepts of reproduction is not the main reason that adolescent girls and even adult women get pregnant. Instead, females get pregnant often because they want to have children. Although some may later decide that they have made a mistake, most women choose to engage in unprotected sex despite what they may have learned in sex education classes. A better way of preventing unwanted pregnancy and lowering rates of teen sexual intercourse starts in the home. The development of strong values is more important than in-school sex education, abstinence-only or otherwise.

A [2007] study by the Mathematica Policy Research Institute concluded that abstinence-education programs do not delay the age at which teens first have sex. The response from the left was predictable: "We've spent billions of dollars and we don't have anything to show for it, so it is time for this Congress to fund programs that work," William Smith at the Sexuality Information and Education Council of the U.S. told *USA Today*. The study's conclusion that teens in abstinence-only programs were no less likely than their peers to use contraception apparently didn't faze Mr. Smith. (Somehow they're getting "sexuality information" without benefit of formal education.)

Families should teach values; public schools should stick to reading and math.

The right, not surprisingly, remains unconvinced by the report: "Fortunately, there are 15 other studies (most appearing in peer-reviewed journals) showing that abstinence programs are effective in reducing youth sexual activity," said Robert Rector of the Heritage Foundation. Mr. Rector noted a few factors he saw as flaws in the study, including that the abstinence classes under examination were offered only to children ages 10 to 13 and there was no follow-up after that.

No follow-up? A skeptic might wonder just how many classroom hours it will take to get the abstinence message across. Teaching adolescents how not to get pregnant should take about as much time as teaching them how to make a peanut-butter sandwich. Whether you instruct them to refrain from intercourse altogether or to use a form of contraception, sex education is not an intellectual problem. And Mr. Rector does recognize this. "Abstinence education also teaches that sexual activity should involve love, intimacy and commitment, and that these qualities are most likely to be found in marriage," he explains. If the Mathematica study proves correct, though, Mr. Rector can find comfort in the fact that its results confirm a basic conservative principle—families should teach values; public schools should stick to reading and math.

And what do the contraceptive-education folks spend their class hours on? As Barbara Dafoe Whitehead explained in a 1994 article in the *Atlantic*, sex education "sweeps across disciplines, taking up the biology of reproduction, the psychology of relationships, the sociology of the family and the sexology of masturbation and massage." The sex-ed crowd doesn't only want to prevent teen pregnancy and disease. It wants kids to feel comfortable about their sexuality.

That's something that can't happen, of course, without "information." The left charges that the right wants to keep kids in some kind of religiously inspired ignorance about their bodies. Here is a typical opinion of abstinence education offered by a sex-ed teacher in the galleys of Tom Perotta's forthcoming novel *The Abstinence Teacher*. "Shameless fear mongering, backed up by half-truths and bogus examples and inflammatory rhetoric." Again, though, it would be hard to imagine that the vast majority of teens who get pregnant today do so because they don't understand how not to.

Women Get Pregnant Because They Want To

Yet the "information" mantra continues. In a recent column Atul Gawande, a guest op-ed writer for the *New York Times*, even went so far as to say that adult women get pregnant unintentionally because they don't understand how to use birth control properly. "The trouble appears to be blindness to how easy it is to get pregnant and what it takes to make birth control really work."

A surgeon, Dr. Gawande was trying to find a medically plausible explanation for the sad fact that there are 1.3 million abortions in the U.S. and that about half are performed on women over the age of 25. It's an interesting problem. Three-quarters of American women tell pollsters that they think abortion is morally wrong in at least some circumstances. The most common exceptions mentioned—rape, incest and life of the mother—are in fact the least common reasons women have abortions. So what gives?

Maybe the answer is obvious: Women get pregnant because they want to have babies. As Kay S. Hymowitz, author of *Marriage and Caste in America*, puts it, "There isn't really a bright line between wanted and unwanted pregnancies." There are plenty of women who become careless about birth control on purpose. Whether they're suburban professionals with two sons who really want a daughter or poor inner-city women who hope their boyfriends will stay around if there is a child in the picture, women will often subvert their better judgment to fulfill a biological urge.

This is not the sort of sentiment that sits well with feminists—or with anyone, for that matter, who believes women are the ones thinking with their heads instead of their hormones. But according to the Guttmacher Institute, there are about three million unintended pregnancies in the U.S. every year, and six in 10 U.S. women having abortions are already mothers. More than half intend to have (more) children in the future. These ladies know exactly how one gets pregnant, and how one does not.

Education, it seems, can do only so much.

Which brings us back to Dr. Gawande's dilemma. A disproportionate number of poor women, it turns out, account for those 1.3 million abortions every year. But this is not because, as Mr. Smith might argue, they are disproportionately uneducated when it comes to sex and birth control. It's because, having decided to "unintentionally" get pregnant, they quickly realize that having a baby is not feasible. Whereas the suburban married professional might have to stretch her family's income a bit further to make room for an unplanned third child, the poor single woman might find herself without a man in her life four months into her pregnancy and determine that raising a child by herself just isn't an option.

Mr. Rector could conclude that the poor woman simply needs a stronger education in values. But that is not quite right, either. However unfortunate her decision to abort, the poor woman probably knows that it would be better for everyone involved if her child were raised in a stable two-parent household. She just hoped that she would have one in time. Education, it seems, can do only so much.

2

Schools Should Educate Teens About Sex

Peter Cumper

Peter Cumper is a law professor at the University of Leicester, England.

Sex education classes are essential for the well being of young people and society in general, but determining the best way of ensuring that children receive this education is difficult. While parental rights should be respected, the best interests of children should supplant those rights. Given that the number of unplanned pregnancies and sexually transmitted diseases continues to climb, sex education is not negotiable. In addition, adolescents should have a say in whether or not they attend sex education classes because it affects their futures.

There are few issues that generate as much controversy in the school curriculum as sex and relationship education (SRE). Typically of interest to a wide range of parties, such as academics, healthcare professionals, politicians, pressure groups and religious organisations, SRE inevitably raises a host of complex moral, educational and political issues. Perhaps the most contentious of these is the extent to which a balance can be struck between the rights of children and the responsibilities of parents in the provision of SRE in the classroom.

In the past, sex and relationship issues were seldom a matter for debate. The rights of parents were paramount, and the

Peter Cumper, "'Let's Talk About Sex': Balancing Children's Rights and Parental Responsibilities," *Legal Studies*, vol. 26, no. 1, March 2006, pp. 88–108. Copyright © 2006 Basil Blackwell Ltd. Reproduced by permission of Blackwell Publishers.

interests of children in the area of sexual health, as elsewhere, were largely ignored. Parents have, therefore, long been regarded as being ultimately responsible for the upbringing of their children, and the related principle of parental choice in the field of education has been widely recognised as a fundamental human right. In recent decades, however, the legal relationship between parents and children has undergone a 'quiet revolution'. The idea that parents' interests should *always* prevail over those of their children has been rejected, and today judges subscribe to the view that 'parental rights are derived from parental duty and exist only so long as they are needed for the protection . . . of the child'. With young people increasingly being accorded the right to have their wishes taken into account on matters affecting their upbringing, it is perhaps not surprising that the rights of the child have been recognised under both domestic and international law.

It is in the interests of society in general . . . for every secondary school pupil to be in receipt of sex education.

Yet, while young people are increasingly consulted on matters that concern them in contemporary England and Wales (where every maintained secondary school is required to offer SRE classes), sex education policies are still formulated by teachers, schools' governing bodies and, to a lesser extent, parents. A graphic illustration of this exclusion of young people from the decision-making process is the fact that parents in England and Wales retain the statutory right to withdraw their children from SRE lessons that fall outside of the national curriculum. Although fewer than 1% of parents exercise such a right of withdrawal, this proportion nevertheless amounts to a sizeable number of young people who will enter adult life without having received formal school-based instruction on matters that the state deems necessary for their fellow citizens. Accordingly, a consensus has emerged that the interests of young people would be best served if parents were no longer able to withdraw their children from SRE classes. . . .

Building Bridges—Suggested Reforms

While there has been disagreement in the past as to the exact parameters of children's rights, there is a consensus today that the wishes of young people are not absolute and instead must be balanced against a number of other factors. These may, for example, include the need to protect the child from harm, as well as according respect to the wishes of parents and taking into account the general interests of society. Thus, even though commentators have recognised that young people may argue, say, for the freedom to choose their own lifestyles or assert rights against their parents, there is also acceptance of the fact that the child's autonomy is qualified. Accordingly, notwithstanding the increasing recognition of the rights of children, it has been argued that 'to see sex education purely as a matter of the child's choice or autonomy would be an unbalanced and one-dimensional view'.

Mindful of such considerations, the challenge of striking a fair balance between the rights of children, the responsibilities of parents and the duties of the state in the provision of SRE is formidable. In seeking to reconcile these apparently competing interests, it is, however, suggested that the governing principle must always be what is in the best interests of the child. Given that teenage birth rates are much higher in Britain than in any of our European neighbours, a record which even the Prime Minster has called 'shameful', there is certainly a strong case for arguing that it is in the interests of society in general, and of young people in particular, for *every* secondary school pupil to be in receipt of sex education. Such a view appears to be held by a number of healthcare professionals, journalists and parliamentarians, all having recently called for the removal of the 'parental veto' in the area of SRE.

Of course, determinations of what constitutes the best interests of the child are usually influenced by considerations such as one's culture and . . . cultural and religious sensibilities are likely to ensure that any attempt to dilute the parental influence in the field of SRE will be fiercely resisted by a minority of conservative parents. In view of the recent acknowledgment from the Children's Minister, Beverley Hughes, that the support of parents is crucial if the government is to succeed in tackling the alarmingly high rates of teenage pregnancy, care must be taken not to risk alienating those parents who are wary of SRE. Below, I seek to outline a workable compromise that will, on the one hand, accord recognition to the rights of the child yet, on the other, assuage the fears of concerned parents.

Research indicates that the most successful sex education programmes require the full participation and cooperation of all parents.

The Rights of the Child

My first proposal for reform is that young people should, at the very least, have a formal say in any attempt by a parent to remove his/her child from SRE lessons. In giving parents this power of withdrawal, ministers appear to have been confident that parents would almost always 'take full account' of their children's wishes. Irrespective of whether such an assumption is reasonable, it can be argued that international human rights law already puts schools under a duty to obtain the views of every young person before s/he is withdrawn from sex education classes. Of course, policy makers may be wary of supporting a reform that could potentially set children against their parents, and hidden family pressures are likely to militate against anything other than a handful of young people expressing opinions at variance with those of their parents in the field of sex education. Nevertheless, as long as parents retain the right to take their children out of SRE lessons, the views of those young people who are directly affected should be formally recorded and they ought to be informed that, irrespective of parental objection, they are free to borrow a school's teaching materials on sex education.

My second suggestion is that respect for the rights of young people demands that new age restrictions are introduced, whereby attendance at SRE lessons becomes compulsory for *all* pupils once they have reached a specified age—say 13. This proposal would have a number of advantages. To begin with, it would remove the bizarre anomaly that 16-year-old pupils in maintained schools, who lawfully can have sexual intercourse and even get married, may be withdrawn from SRE classes by their parents. Moreover, it would reflect the fact that the age of sexual consent is fluid and is lower than 16 in a number of other European countries. In addition, it would fashion a compromise, since no adolescent (aged 13 and above) would be denied access to information about sex and relationships, while the influence of parents over the education of infants and young children would be retained.

Thirdly, for as long as the parental right to remove a child from SRE lessons survives, the interests of young people demand that, first, parents should be required to explain their concerns to the school before exercising their power of withdrawal. Currently, a parent who wishes to prevent his/her child from attending SRE lessons is under no such duty, but, as has been argued elsewhere, 'there is a case for demanding that acceptable reasons are provided'. Inevitably, this proposal would be synonymous with controversy and, while an 'acceptable' reason would presumably be a genuine religious or philosophical objection to the provision of SRE, there would have to be a mechanism in place so that disputes between parents and schools could be resolved. Any such requirement, whereby appropriate reasons would have to be given prior to withdrawing one's child from SRE lessons, would undeniably be difficult to implement, but it would, at the very least, force parents to reconsider their objections to sex education and could provide schools with an opportunity to tackle previously unaddressed parental concerns. The interests of young people demand that, as long as the parental veto is retained in the field of SRE, the burden is on the parent to justify removing a child from sex education classes.

Assuaging the Fears of Parents

For reasons discussed earlier, a number of parents of a mainly conservative religious disposition are wary of SRE. Yet research indicates that the most successful sex education programmes require the full participation and cooperation of all parents. Therefore, rather than focusing on the child at the exclusion of the parent, it is important to explore a number of ways in which bridges can be built between all of the interested parties.

Some parents would, for example, be less wary of sex education lessons if boys and girls were to be taught SRE in separate classes, with pupils (subject to the availability of staff and resources) receiving instruction from a teacher of their own sex. This suggestion, which has been supported in principle by the Commons Health Select Committee, appears to have also received the backing of a number of academics and minority faith leaders, as well as young people generally. Moreover, with the incorporation of the European Convention on Human Rights, Protocol 1, Art 2 into domestic law, it seems that the state may now be under a duty to respect the wishes of *parents* who are in favour of SRE being taught in single-sex classes. For example, *R v Newham London Borough Coucil, ex p K*, it was held that a local education authority was required to take into account the religious and philosophical convictions of a Muslim father, who wanted to send his daughter to a single-sex school. In the same way, it could be argued that, subject to considerations of cost, the state is under a duty to ensure that respect is accorded to the wishes of parents who want their children only to receive SRE in classes with pupils of the same sex. Although disagreement on the extent to which Protocol 1, Art 2 imposes a positive obligation on the state in the field of SRE is inevitable, the introduction of this reform would, at the very least, be a relatively inexpensive way of taking account of the religious and cultural sensibilities of some parents.

Teachers Must Be Trained

The concerns of conservative parents are also likely to be allayed if they are confident that highly trained teachers or healthcare professionals are responsible for the provision of sex education. While there is no evidence to suggest that most schools are anything other than conscientious when they offer SRE lessons, many teachers have acknowledged that they are poorly equipped for this task. The importance of the teacher's role in this area is clear, and both the Commons Health Select Committee and Ofsted [Office for Standards in Education, Children's Services and Skills] have recognised that teachers who are well trained in the subject typically lead the most effective SRE lessons. However, the Sex Education Forum has claimed that 'very few professionals' have the knowledge and skills to respond confidently to young people's questions in this field, and considerations such as these have led the British Medical Association to call for an increase in the number of Health Promotion Officers working in schools. In an ideal world, every school would certainly have its own specialist nurse to offer advice on health matters generally and SRE in particular. However, in the light of the shortcomings of the nation's healthcare system, this is a forlorn hope. In its place, however, there are a number of ways in which effective health education strategies could be promoted. There should, for example, be an increase in the number of specialist SRE teachers in schools; or failing that, schemes such as the 'pooling [of] teachers across a consortium of schools within a local authority' should be adopted. Assistance could also be given to teachers about how they can most effectively tackle issues relating to sexuality; and, perhaps most controversially, formal SRE classes could be supplemented by sessions in which specially trained older children offer guidance on sex and relationships to younger pupils, since there is evidence that some teenagers are more receptive to lessons led by peer educators than to those given by their teachers.

Lastly, the introduction of additional measures to encourage parents to discuss with their children many of the issues covered in SRE lessons could partly demystify sex education and might allay the fears of some parents. Although the government has recognised the need to 'encourage parents to talk to their children about sex and relationships', further changes are necessary. For example, parents could be encouraged to attend SRE workshops run by healthcare professionals; schemes ought to be encouraged whereby parents are offered the loan of SRE materials for use at home with their children; and an online sex education programme for parents to access at home could be set up, to supplement other useful sex education sites on the Internet. Of course, it would be naive to exaggerate the possible impact of such reforms—there will always be a handful of parents (often fathers) who, out of indifference, embarrassment or wilful neglect, refuse to provide sex education to their children. This may be compounded in communities where sex 'is not a subject which is talked about openly within the family', although it is myth that SRE is a taboo subject in only minority-faith families. Yet with cases of sexually transmitted diseases continuing to rise, and an alarmingly high number of very young girls continuing to fall pregnant, further action is urgently needed. At the very least it must be said that, as long as parents retain the right to withdraw their children from SRE lessons, the state is under a special duty to support initiatives which ensure that *all* young people are in receipt of such information in the home. . . .

3

Abstinence-Only Education Violates Students' Rights

American Civil Liberties Union

American Civil Liberties Union (ACLU) is a national organization dedicated to protecting civil rights.

Federally funded abstinence-only programs are not only ineffective at reducing teen pregnancy and sexually transmitted disease rates, but they infringe upon students' First Amendment rights. Because these programs censor essential health information, they put teens at risk. In addition, the overtly religious focus of most of these programs clearly violates the constitutional rule which guarantees the separation of church and state. Also, gay and lesbian students, who have no right to future marriage possibilities, are given no options under abstinence-only-until-marriage programs.

Despite statistics that demonstrate a high level of sexual activity among U.S. teens, Congress has allocated well over half a billion dollars since 1997 for educational programs that focus exclusively on abstinence and censor other information that can help young people make responsible, healthy, and safe decisions about sexual activity. Mounting evidence reveals that these abstinence-only programs are ineffective and factually inaccurate. Nevertheless, in recent years, federal lawmakers have steadily increased federal funding for abstinence-only-until-marriage programs to more than $165 million an-

American Civil Liberties Union, "ACLU Memo to Interested Persons Regarding Abstinence-Only-Until-Marriage Programs," *ACLU*, March 1, 2006. Reproduced by permission

nually. In contrast, no federal funds are dedicated to supporting comprehensive sexual education programs that teach both abstinence and contraceptive use. The ACLU strongly opposes abstinence-only-until-marriage programs, which raise serious civil liberties and public health concerns.

While the discussion of abstinence is an important component of any educational program about human sexuality, federally funded programs that focus *exclusively* on abstinence raise serious health and civil liberties concerns. The programs censor information essential to teen's health, trample constitutional rights of free expression, create a hostile environment for lesbian and gay youth, and often unconstitutionally entangle the government with religion.

Federal Funding Programs

Three principal federal programs fund abstinence-only education:

- *Section 510 of the 1996 Welfare Reform Act.* This 1996 law, known as the Personal Responsibility and Work Opportunity Reconciliation Act of 1996 (PRWORA), provided $250 million over five years for programs with the "exclusive purpose" of promoting abstinence. Funding has since been extended at a level of $50 million per year. The law sets forth a narrow eight-point definition of abstinence-only education.

- *Special Programs of Regional and National Significance (SPRANS).* SPRANS is the largest funding source of abstinence-only education. In fiscal year 2001, its first year of funding, SPRANS recipients received $20 million in grants. Funding under this program has increased dramatically: For fiscal year 2006, for example, $109 million was appropriated.

- *The Adolescent Family Life Act (AFLA).* This 1981 legislation was passed "to promote self discipline and other prudent approaches to the problem of adolescent premarital sexual relations" to teens. For fiscal year 2006, approximately $13 million was appropriated for abstinence-only education.

All three programs require recipients to adhere to the eight-point definition of abstinence-only education contained in Section 510. Grantees under SPRANS must teach all eight points of this definition. Until this year, grantees under Section 510, while not permitted to provide information inconsistent with any of the definition's points, were not required to teach all eight points. However, in March 2005 the Administration for Children and Families (ACF) issued new guidance for the Section 510 program that seemingly eliminated this flexibility. The new guidance "strongly encourage[s]" states to place equal emphasis on each element of the definition. Grantees under AFLA are not required to teach all eight points but may not provide information that is inconsistent with any point.

Abstinence-Only Programs Are Ineffective

A growing body of evidence demonstrates that many abstinence-only programs are simply ineffective. As an independent, federally funded evaluation of the abstinence-only education programs authorized under the 1996 welfare reform law concluded, there is "no definitive research [linking] the abstinence education legislation with" the downward trend in "the percentage of teens reporting that they have had sex."

Recipients of federal abstinence-only funds operate under a gag order that censors the communication of vital information.

More troubling, the evidence suggests that some programs actually *increase* risk-taking behaviors among sexually active teens. A recent study of teens in virginity-pledge programs—which encourage students to pledge to abstain from sex until marriage—found that virginity pledgers, while more likely to delay first intercourse, are less likely than non-pledgers to protect themselves from sexually-transmitted infections ("STIs") at first intercourse. Moreover, pledgers are more likely to engage in alternative sexual behaviors in order to preserve their virginity: among virgins—defined as those who have not had vaginal intercourse—male pledgers are four times more likely to have anal sex and male and female pledgers are six times more likely to have oral sex than non-pledgers. Despite these risky practices, pledgers are less likely to seek and obtain STI-related health care.

In sharp contrast, the overwhelming weight of evidence shows that comprehensive programs providing information about both abstinence and contraception do help reduce sexual risk-taking, pregnancy, and the risk of STIs among teens. Many of these comprehensive programs have been shown to "delay the onset of sex, reduce the frequency of sex, reduce the number of sexual partners among teens, or increase the use of condoms and other forms of contraception" among sexually active teens.

Abstinence-Only Education Censors Information

Recipients of federal abstinence-only funds operate under a gag order that censors the communication of vital information. To receive funds, grantees must offer programs with the "exclusive purpose" of teaching the benefits of abstinence. Recipients of federal funds may not provide a participating adolescent with any information that is inconsistent with the narrow eight-point definition of abstinence-only education. Consequently, recipients of abstinence-only dollars may not advocate contraceptive use or teach contraceptive methods—even if a teen directly asks for this information—except to emphasize their failure rates.

The government's mandate thus censors the transmission of vital information about human sexuality and reproduction. And in the schools, this funding serves to force many teachers to avoid providing educational information they consider valuable to teens: a 1999 nationally representative survey of 7th–12th grade teachers in the five specialties most often responsible for sex education found that a strong majority believed sexuality education courses should cover birth control methods (93.4%), factual information about abortion (89%), where to go for birth control (88.8%), the correct way to use a condom (82%), and sexual orientation (77.8%), among other topics.

Abstinence-Only Education Endangers Teens' Health

Statistics reveal that teens need information about contraception and sexual health: nearly two-thirds of all high school seniors in the U.S. have had sexual intercourse; approximately 822,000 pregnancies occurred among 15–19 year old women in 2000; and each year, approximately 9.1 million 15—24 year olds are infected with STIs. Abstinence-only programs, however, leave teens without information critical to protecting their health and preventing pregnancy.

These programs violate the First Amendment's guarantee of the separation between church and state by using taxpayer money to endorse religious beliefs and underwrite religious activities.

Worse still, federally funded abstinence-only programs can actually leave teens with *inaccurate* information. A recent study conducted by the United States House of Representatives Committee on Government Reform found that eleven of the thirteen abstinence-only curricula used by SPRANS programs "contain major errors and distortions about public health information," including HIV and other STD [sexually transmitted disease] prevention, pregnancy prevention, and condom effectiveness. These eleven curricula are used in 25 states by state health departments, school districts, and hospitals. Another recent study, conducted by Case Western University, found that abstinence-only programs contain patently false information about contraceptive effectiveness rates, "inflated statistics" regarding abortion, and "false and inaccurate information" about STD transmission.

Teens need a source of comprehensive and accurate sex education, however. In reality, many teens are not getting the information they need from their parents. As one study found, only half of young women 18–19, and just over a third of men this age, have talked with a parent about birth control.

For these reasons, federally funded abstinence-only programs run counter to the recommendation of major medical organizations, including the American Public Health Association, the American Academy of Pediatrics, and the National Campaign to Prevent Teen Pregnancy. Because of their interest in teens' health, these organizations have advocated for and/or endorsed comprehensive sexuality education.

> *These programs violate . . . the separation between church and state by using taxpayer money to endorse religious beliefs and underwrite religious activities.*

Abstinence-Only Programs Harm Gay Youth

Federally funded abstinence-only programs marginalize gay and lesbian students and stigmatize homosexuality by requiring that no program teach a message inconsistent with the view that a "mutually faithful monogamous relationship in [the] context of marriage is the expected standard of human sexual activity." Such a message rejects the idea of sexual intimacy for lesbians and gays, ignores their need for critical information about protecting themselves from STIs in same-sex relationships, and creates a hostile learning environment. Indeed, a recent study of Ohio abstinence-only programs concluded that "one of the greatest flaws of abstinence programs is their inherent exclusion of [lesbian, gay, bisexual, and transgender] youth."

A recent review of the leading abstinence-only curricula found that most address same-sex sexual behavior only within the context of promiscuity and disease, and several are overtly hostile to lesbians and gay men. For example, in its parent-teacher guide, an abstinence-only program called "Facing Reality" instructs educators to teach students that homosexuals with AIDS are now suffering for the "choices" they made regarding their sexual orientation.

By positioning sex within a heterosexual marriage as the "standard" for sexual activity and teaching that STIs are a form of moral punishment for homosexuality, abstinence-only programs undermine efforts to educate students about protecting their health and create a hostile learning environment for lesbian and gay students.

Violation of the Separation of Church and State

In violation of First Amendment guarantees, many federally funded abstinence-only programs contain religious teachings about proper sexual behavior and values. These programs violate the First Amendment's guarantee of the separation between church and state by using taxpayer money to endorse religious beliefs and underwrite religious activities.

The Supreme Court has made clear that "[u]nder our system the choice has been made that government is to be entirely excluded from the area of religious instruction and churches excluded from the affairs of government. The Constitution decrees that religion must be a private matter for the individual, the family, and the institutions of private choice. . . ." Indeed, as Justice O'Connor stated in *Bowen v.*

Kendrick, a case challenging the constitutionality of the Adolescent Family Life Act and its appropriation of funds for abstinence-only education, "public funds may not be used to endorse [a] religious message."

Although federal funding guidelines do not permit abstinence-only grantees to convey overt religious messages or to impose religious viewpoints, in practice, many of these programs do precisely that. In 2002, the ACLU challenged the use of taxpayer dollars to support religious activities in the Louisiana Governor's Program (GPA) on Abstinence, a program run on federal and state funds. The GPA funded programs that, among other things, presented "Christ-centered" theater skits, held a religious youth revival, and produced radio shows that "share abstinence as part of the gospel message." A federal district court found the GPA funds were being used to convey religious messages and advance religion, in violation of the Constitution's requirement of separation of church and state, and ordered Louisiana officials to stop this misuse of taxpayer dollars. The case was on appeal when the parties settled.

There is good reason to believe that these violations are occurring in other federally funded programs as well. For example, the ACLU recently filed a federal suit, *ACLU v. Leavitt*, challenging, on First Amendment establishment clause grounds, the use of federal dollars to support an overtly religious abstinence-only program called The Silver Ring Thing. The Silver Ring Thing has been awarded more than one million dollars in federal money over the last three years. During the "Silver Ring Thing's" flagship three-hour program, members testify about how accepting Jesus Christ improved their lives, quote Bible passages, and urge audience members to ask the Lord Jesus Christ to come into their lives. In addition, the official silver ring of the program is inscribed with a reference to the biblical verse "1 Thess. 4:3–4," which reads "God wants you to be holy, so you should keep clear of all sexual sin. Then each of you will control your body and live in holiness and honor." As the ACLU's lawsuit argued, the use of taxpayer dollars to fund such overtly religious programs is flatly unconstitutional. Apparently, the Department of Justice agreed. As a result of the ACLU's lawsuit, federal officials suspended federal funding of the Silver Ring Thing. And, in February 2006, the ACLU announced a settlement with the Department of Health and Human Services (HHS); under the terms of the settlement, HHS agreed it will not fund the Silver Ring Thing as the program is currently structured, that any future funding is contingent on program's compliance with federal law prohibiting the use of federal funds to support religious activities, and that HHS will monitor any future grants to the program.

Because abstinence-only programs endanger young people's health and run afoul of constitutional protections, the ACLU strongly opposes their continued funding.

4

Comprehensive Sex Education Is Inappropriate and Harmful

National Abstinence Education Association

National Abstinence Education Association is a nonprofit organization that advocates for abstinence-only education through education initiatives and lobbying activities.

The most common form of sex education classes in the United States is referred to as comprehensive sex education (CSE), or "abstinence plus." Although proponents of such programs argue that they provide the most factual information to teens, a close examination of their literature reveals otherwise. Teens enrolled in these classes are given false information about how pregnancy and sexually transmitted diseases can be avoided and may actually be encouraged to engage in activities that could lead to sexual intercourse. CSE curriculum is harmful to young people and should be replaced with abstinence-only-until-marriage programs.

Across America, so-called "comprehensive sex education" (CSE—also referred to as "abstinence plus") is the dominant sex education message presented to teens in schools. Unfortunately, few Americans are familiar with the actual content of these classroom curricula. This analysis serves to expose the real nature of comprehensive or "abstinence-plus" sex education and underscore why this approach is harmful to our nation's teens. Direct quotes will be taken from some of the

National Abstinence Education Association, "Straight From The Source: What So Called 'Comprehensive' Sex Education Teaches to America's Youth," *National Abstinence Education Association*, June 2007. Reproduced by permission.

most widely recommended comprehensive sex education curricula, of which many are sourced from the recently released HHS [Health and Human Services] report on this topic. The students targeted by these curricula range from children as young as 10 to 12 years old (middle school students) through high school age youth.

Not a single CSE text encourages teens to delay sex until at least out of high school, much less, waiting until marriage.

In recent years, proponents of comprehensive sex education have attempted to "rebrand" their programs by renaming them "abstinence plus." Both terms, however, are significantly misleading. Regardless of what they are called, "comprehensive" or "abstinence plus" programs spend minimal time actually promoting the importance of abstinence. Instead, there is a presumption and often an encouragement of sexual activity, as well as a narrow focus on promoting contraceptive use, even though the majority of teens today are not having sex. Further, the content of CSE programs is decidedly at odds with what the majority of American parents want their children to be taught. . . .

Dangerous Distortions and Inaccurate Information

The overall message delivered to students is one that dangerously states or [implies] that sex can be made safe and without consequences as long as a condom is used. According to the CDC [Centers for Disease Control and Prevention], condom use reduces but does not eliminate the transmission of any STD [sexually transmitted disease]. Yet comprehensive sex education repeatedly fails to communicate this distinction, implying that if "protection" is used, sex is "safe." Further, numerous studies have shown that at best, only about 50 percent of adults use condoms consistently. Yet CSE programs exaggerate the level of "protection" offered by condoms by quoting "perfect use" failure rates instead of the higher, more realistic "typical use" failure rates. One text even warns facilitators not to mention any limitations on condom effectiveness to students. This censorship is alarming, particularly when one realizes that the decisions students make regarding their sexual health can have lifelong and even fatal consequences.

CSE programs inaccurately promote some non-intercourse sexual activities are "safe" while ignoring the possibility of skin to skin transmission of certain STDs. This approach is misleading, dangerous and puts vulnerable youth at risk.

Examples from Comprehensive Sex Education Curricula:

- "Remind students that there are 2 ways to avoid pregnancy and HIV infection: say no to sex, or use protection"

  INACCURATE: Only abstinence provides 100% protection against pregnancy and the sexual transmission of HIV.

- "Safer sex will prevent HIV infection. . . . If HIV infection can indeed be prevented, then there is nothing to fear"

  INACCURATE: Only abstinence provides 100% protection against the sexual transmission of HIV.

- "Latex condoms are the only form of birth control that can prevent pregnancy and sexually transmitted disease, including HIV"

  INACCURATE: Only abstinence provides 100% protection against pregnancy and the transmission of STDs.

- ". . . any behavior that involves exposure to blood, semen, or vaginal secretions can transmit STDs, including HIV."

INACCURATE: Skin to skin contact is all that is necessary for some STDs, such as HPV and herpes, to be transmitted. . . .

CSE programs inaccurately present an ambiguous definition of abstinence, with some stating that abstinence is "anything you want it to mean."

Understating the Overwhelming Advantages of Abstinence

Not a single CSE text encourages teens to delay sex until at least out of high school, much less, waiting until marriage. Further, CSE programs make continual suggestions that abstinence and sex with contraception are equally viable options, which is a violation of basic medical accuracy and is dangerously misleading. For example, among typical couples using condoms for birth control, 15 percent per year become pregnant, versus 0 percent for those choosing abstinence. Such misinformation not only withholds the overwhelming advantage of the abstinence choice but censors important information teens need to make truly informed decisions for their sexual health.

Examples from Comprehensive Sex Education Curricula:

- "There are only 2 ways to avoid pregnancy and HIV— not having sexual intercourse, or consistently using protection"

- A handout lists two methods that "protects for pregnancy and HIV". They are abstinence and a latex condom.

- "Practicing safer sex, including abstinence, is not something anyone can do without the cooperation of his or her partner." . . .

Teens who become sexually active often express regret over their decision indicating that sex is more than a physical act that one can separate from the emotional or psychological dimension of a person. Indeed numerous recent studies document the emotional effect of sex on teens, particularly girls, with even the most nuanced arguments admitting that emotional distress associated with teen dating experiences is minimized when sex is not part of the relationship. Unfortunately, comprehensive sex education completely ignores the holistic nature of sexual activity, including the potential negative emotional consequences for teens that become sexually active.

Promoting Provocative (vs. Preventative) Alternatives to Intercourse

CSE programs contain an explicit promotion of alternatives to intercourse by suggesting allegedly "safe" "outercourse activities." The presentation of these examples as "safe" is medically inaccurate because it ignores the possibility of skin-to-skin transmission of disease. Further, these suggestions represent blatant advocacy for "gateway" sexual activities that create arousal for the very intercourse they are purportedly designed to prevent. This approach ignores the natural momentum such intimacy produces and fails to teach students reasonable and safe boundaries within relationships.

Examples from Comprehensive Sex Education Curricula:

- "Outercourse allows people to express their sexuality in many ways, remain abstinent, and avoid the risks of sexually transmitted infection and unplanned pregnancy."

- "Write *BENEFITS OF OUTERCOURSE* on the board/easel paper and ask participants to brainstorm all the advantages of outercourse as compared to intercourse."

- One activity, entitled "The Endless Possibilities of Outercourse" lists all areas of the body, from head to toe and then asks students to brainstorm sexual activities they could engage in with each body part. Suggested kinds of touch include: "stroking, petting, squeezing, hugging, sucking, nuzzling, licking, and kissing" . . .

Providing Ambiguous, Inaccurate Definitions of "Abstinence"

The U.S. Department of Health and Human Services Administration for Children and Families define sexual abstinence as "voluntarily choosing not to engage in sexual activity until marriage. Sexual activity refers to any type of genital contact or sexual stimulation between two persons including, but not limited to, sexual intercourse." This definition assures the avoidance of ALL risk associated with sexual activity.

In contrast, CSE programs inaccurately present an ambiguous definition of abstinence, with some stating that abstinence is "anything you want it to mean." Often, there is no clear risk-avoidance definition given and students are encouraged to define abstinence in a way that feels right for them. Further, many of the titillating "outercourse" activities are presented as ways to remain "abstinent." This is not education but rather abdication of the role of guiding youth with the full information they need to make personally informed decisions based on sound reasoning and facts.

Examples from Comprehensive Sex Education Curricula:

- "Imagine someone has decided to be *abstinent*. According to your own definition of "abstinence," circle the following sexual behaviors you believe a person can engage in and *still be abstinent*." Among the choices: "reading erotic literature; cuddling naked; mutual masturbation; showering together; watching porn; talking sexy."

- Abstinence may include "sexually pleasurable things without having intercourse (e.g. masturbation, kissing, talking, massaging, having fantasies, etc.)" . . .

Presentation of Explicit and Inappropriate Content

CSE programs use explicit demonstrations to teach contraception usage skills. The commentary accompanying many of these demonstrations refers to sexual activity as "fun" in a way that trivializes the inherent risks along with a tone of tacit endorsement that communicates sexual activity among teens as "normal" and expected. The explicit nature of these demonstrations crosses the line between factual education and actual provocative promotion, demonstrating a violation of the need to educate not advocate. . . .

Examples from Comprehensive Sex Education Curricula:

- "If you aren't sexually active now, one day you probably will be. I believe this information about sexual response is important for you to learn. It might make you feel a little uncomfortable at first as I go through it, but let's all learn together and have fun." An explicit, excessively detailed step-by-step instructive tutorial on the sex process and manipulations of genitalia is then given. This explanation is specifically meant for those who are not yet sexually active in order to make them "aware."

- "Give each participant a condom and lubricant. Each participant should practice putting condoms on their fingers. Then let them give you a demonstration." . . .

- "Explain that with their partners, they should go to a local market or drugstore to gather information about protective products, such as condoms and vaginal spermicides. After finding the protective products they should complete the homework, identifying what types of protection are available, how much they cost, and whether they are accessible to teens who may want to purchase them. Finally, they should decide how comfortable they would be buying protection in that store and whether they would recommend that store to a friend."

- "Visit or call a clinic: . . . Besides learning what services are offered at local family planning clinics, this homework assignment asks students to rate their comfort level while at the clinic" . . .

Undermining the Role of Parents

CSE programs repeatedly inform teens that they can acquire birth control and reproductive services without their parent's knowledge or consent. While this information may be true, it is inappropriate to tacitly encourage youth to circumvent parental awareness when going to "family" planning clinics. Very little curricula content in CSE programs promote teen and parental communication regarding sexuality issues. Along with this omission is the repeated suggestive instruction that decisions about sex are entirely personal and therefore little advocacy is given to seek or confer with the advice or values of parents. By promoting this unbalanced emphasis on personal autonomy, the role of parents and their values can be easily marginalized and largely ignored by youth. Because of the serious nature of sexual health issues, including the use of prescribed medication and other "reproductive services" offered at family planning clinics, it is extremely important that parental involvement is encouraged.

Examples from Comprehensive Sex Education Curricula:

- "Clarify that teens can obtain many services without parent/guardian permission, such as HIV, other STD and pregnancy testing, or access to condoms and other birth control."

- "Teenagers can obtain birth control pills from family planning clinics and doctors without permission from a parent"

- "You do not need a parent's permission to get birth control at a clinic. No one needs to know that you are going to a clinic."

A 2007 Zogby Poll showed that parents support abstinence education over comprehensive sex education. This survey also found that parents want more instruction in abstinence than in contraception. However, CSE programs spend most of the time and emphasis on contraceptive advocacy, demonstration, and usage, an approach that is clearly at odds with what parents desire for their children. Findings from the NAEA Zogby survey include:

Parents prefer abstinence education over comprehensive sex education by a 2 to 1 margin.

- Once they understand what abstinence education actually teaches, 6 out of 10 parents would rather their child receive abstinence education vs. comprehensive sex education. Only 3 out of 10 prefer comprehensive.

Most parents reject comprehensive sex education, which focuses on promoting and demonstrating contraceptive use.

- 2 out of 3 parents think that the importance of the "wait to have sex" message ends up being lost when programs demonstrate and encourage the use of contraception.

- Over half of parents think that promoting and demonstrating condom usage encourages sexual activity.

- 8 out of 10 parents think teens will not use a condom every single time.

- 2 out of 3 parents believe that promoting alternatives to intercourse (such as showering together and mutual masturbation, which are presented in some comprehensive programs) encourages sexual activity.

9 out of 10 parents want teens to be taught about contraception in a manner that is consistent with the approach of abstinence education.

- 9 out of 10 parents think teens should be taught how often condoms fail to prevent pregnancy based upon typical use.

- Over 9 out of 10 parents think that teens should be taught the limitations of condoms in preventing specific STDs.

CSE texts spend, on average, less than 5% of their time on abstinence related topics.

Parents want more funding given to abstinence education than to comprehensive sex education by a 3 to 1 margin.

- 6 out of 10 parents think more government funding should be given to abstinence education vs. comprehensive sex education. Only 2 out of 10 want more funding for comprehensive sex education.

The overwhelming majority of parents want their teens to be abstinent until they are married.

- 9 out of 10 parents agree that being sexually abstinent is best for their child's health and future, with 8 in 10 strongly agreeing.

- 8 out of 10 parents think it's important for their child to wait until they're married to have sex, with 6 in 10 strongly agreeing.

In recent years, "comprehensive" programs have referred to their programs as "abstinence plus," effectively deceiving many parents, schools, youth and the American taxpayer into believing that such programs emphasize abstinence. Most texts refer to abstinence in an understated manner with stunning brevity and lack of emphasis. In fact, CSE texts spend, on average, less than 5% of their time on abstinence related topics.

Examples from Comprehensive Sex Education Curricula

- Activity: "Reviewing important issues on talking with partners about condom use or abstinence" Note: This activity provides two pages of condom usage skills with suggestions such as "remember to talk about how condoms are fun and pleasurable" and only 3 words on abstinence: "abstain from sex"

- "We are pleased to offer you an 'abstinence manual' like no other" Note: The manual never encourages refraining from sexual activity altogether, but rather the discussion of abstinence focuses on what sexual activities may be engaged in without intercourse. Further, this discussion of abstinence acknowledges that "explicit information and communication about sex is essential"

Ineffective Outcomes

According to a report on comprehensive sex education conducted by The US Department of Health and Human Services, there is little evidence that comprehensive programs actually delay the onset of sexual activity. In fact, the majority of programs indicated no delay whatsoever. . . .

Parents have the right to choose what their children are taught, but before they are able to choose, they must be informed of their options. There have been many claims that "comprehensive" sex education programs teach essentially the same message as abstinence programs, and merely add information about contraceptives. A review of CSE curricula shows that this is simply not true. CSE is entirely different from abstinence education, and this fact must be made clear. Sex education programs hide behind a façade of "abstinence" because of the overwhelming support for this approach. Abstinence programs teach abstinence and sex education programs teach sex.

CSE are often referred to as "scientifically and medically accurate" and as "programs that work," but this report reveals the falsehood of these claims. . . .

5

Abstinence-Only Programs Delay Teen Sex

The Institute for Research and Evaluation

The Institute for Research and Evaluation studies the effectiveness of abstinence-only programs in schools and communities across the country.

Finding a means to delay and hopefully prevent intercourse outside of marriage is crucial for the well being of young people and society in general. Mathematica Policy Research, Inc.'s 2007 national study of abstinence programs suggests that teaching abstinence-only sex education is ineffective at reducing adolescent sexual practices. However, the many flaws of this study reveal that effective abstinence-only programs can reduce the overall teen sex rate by as much as half.

The debate about "abstinence" vs. "comprehensive" sex education has been occurring for at least three decades. The common ground that drives these competing approaches is concern about the negative consequences of adolescent sexual activity to the health and well-being of individuals and society. This debate has been re-energized recently by the release of findings from a national study by Mathematica Policy Research, Inc., in which four different abstinence education programs were selected as subjects for a long-term evaluation. This study reported that teen participants in these abstinence programs did not abstain from sexual activity more than nonparticipants, when measured $2^1/_2$ to $5^1/_2$ years after the program ended.

The Institute for Research and Evaluation, "'Abstinence' or 'Comprehensive' Sex Education?—The Mathematica Study in Context," *National Abstinence Education Association*, June 8, 2007. Reproduced by permission.

These results have caused some to conclude that the abstinence approach to preventing teen sexual risk behavior does not work. As one advocate of the "comprehensive" approach stated, "This report should serve as the final verdict on the failure of the abstinence-only industry in this country." Implicit in such statements is the corollary conclusion that the comprehensive sex education approach does work. Neither of these conclusions is supported by the full body of research evidence about "abstinence" and "comprehensive" sex education.

While new evidence can add to the debate, it should never be accepted without scrutiny, and should be viewed alongside the broader base of evidence upon which important policy questions must rely. We have reviewed that body of evidence pertaining to "abstinence" and "comprehensive" approaches to education regarding teen sexual activity. Our institute has also conducted more than 100 evaluations of abstinence education interventions in 30 states over the past 15 years. We draw on this broad base of evidence to share the following observations.

- Many serious problems are associated with adolescent sexual activity.

- Condom interventions have serious limitations.

- When held to the same criteria employed by the Mathematica evaluation, comprehensive sex education programs do not appear to work.

- The Mathematica study, and the four programs it evaluated, cannot be generalized to represent the efficacy of abstinence programs in general.

- Several well designed evaluations of abstinence programs have found significant, long-term reductions in adolescent sexual activity.

- Abstinence education offers benefits to adolescents and society that are not found in the comprehensive sex education approach.

- Abstinence interventions are most effective if they incorporate what has been learned about how to reduce adolescent sexual risk behavior.

We have found that well designed and well implemented abstinence education programs can reduce teen sexual activity by as much as one half for periods of one to two years. For a more detailed discussion of each of our points above, see the pages that follow.

I. Consequences of Teen Sex

In 2005, 63.1% of American adolescents had experienced sexual intercourse by the end of high school. Many serious health and social problems in American society are related to teen sexual activity. These include:

A. *Teen Pregnancy*: One in 13 high-school-age girls becomes pregnant each year in America. Adverse consequences associated with teen pregnancies include abortion, unwed teen parenthood, father absence, poverty, welfare dependence, and the growth of drug abuse, gang culture, and crime.

B. *STDs*: STDs [sexually transmitted diseases] have emerged as a significant threat to adolescent health. The consequences include chronic pelvic pain, genital lesions, lifetime infection, infertility, ectopic (tubal) pregnancy, damage to unborn children, cancer, and in some cases death. Adolescent STD rates are higher than rates for all other age groups. One quarter of sexually active teens have an STD, and adolescent rates for most STDs are on the rise. The growing STD problem has been called a hidden epidemic. The direct medical cost of 9 million new cases of

STDs that occurred among U.S. adolescents and young adults (15–24-year olds) in the year 2000 was estimated at $6.5 billion (in year 2000 dollars).

C. *Poorer Emotional Health*: There is a strong association between sexual activity and poor emotional health for adolescents.

1. Sexually active teens are more than twice as likely as virgin teens to be depressed or attempt suicide. Adolescents report a drop in self-esteem after initiating sexual intercourse, and the majority express regret for becoming sexually active.

2. Sexually experienced teens, especially girls, are much more likely to experience dating violence than their virgin peers, and sexual exploitation (such as statutory rape) and unwanted or forced intercourse/rape are not uncommon among sexually experienced teen girls. In 2005, one out of eight 12th grade girls in the U.S. reported being physically forced to have intercourse against her will.

None of the programs increased the prevalence of consistent condom use (CCU) among adolescents for a period greater than one year.

II. Condom Limitations

Condom use is advocated by many as the best protection for the sexually active from both pregnancy and STD transmission. Yet many consequences of teen sexual activity are not prevented by condom use.

A. Even with consistent and correct use (which is rare), condoms may diminish but do not effectively prevent STDs that are spread through skin-to-skin or skin-to-sore contact. These STDs are on the rise in the adolescent population.

B. After 20-plus years of comprehensive sex education efforts in the U.S., adolescent rates of consistent condom use are not high enough to eliminate the STDs for which condoms are most preventive, such as HIV, let alone STDs for which condoms are least preventive. Adolescents contract one fourth of all new HIV infections. Among sexually active U.S. teens, only 47.8% of males and 27.5% of females report using condoms consistently over a one-year period. Efforts to improve those rates have not proven successful.

C. Consistent condom use cannot prevent the negative emotional impact or the sexual exploitation and sexual violence that are associated with teen sexual activity, as described above.

III. Failure of Comprehensive Programs

When studies are held to the same criteria as the Mathematica evaluation (random assignment, a follow-up period of 2 $\frac{1}{2}$ to 5 $\frac{1}{2}$ years, a high level success criteria), there is ample evidence that condom-based sex education interventions do not work. In the past 20 years, studies evaluating abstinence education programs have been limited in number and in rigor, while during the same time period research on comprehensive sex education has abounded. One recent and thorough summary of this research reviewed 50 well designed evaluation studies of comprehensive sex education programs in the United States, going back to 1990, and included these findings:

A. None of the programs increased the prevalence of consistent condom use (CCU) among adolescents for a period greater than one year. CCU is the only condom measure that approaches the stringent standard of the abstinence measure. Only one program produced a significant increase in the prevalence of CCU that was sustained for a period of one year.

B. Thirteen control trials of comprehensive sex education found no increase in teen condom use for any period of time.

C. Only two comprehensive sex education programs succeeded in improving less stringent measures of teen condom use (not CCU) for a period longer than two years, and none lasted beyond three years.

IV. Mathematica Study Limitations

The Mathematica study, and the four programs it evaluated, cannot be generalized to represent the efficacy of abstinence education or of comprehensive sex education.

A. *The Mathematica Study Did Not Examine Comprehensive Sex Education Programs*: The interpretation some have ascribed to the Mathematica report is that "abstinence programs don't work, therefore we must provide "safer sex" programs to reduce the risks of early sexual activity." The Mathematica study did not draw this conclusion, did not examine safer sex programs, nor suggest that they are the obvious default if abstinence programs are not successful. A substantial number of studies have examined condom-based interventions and can inform policy decisions. In summary, of 50 rigorous studies spanning the past 15 years, only one of them reports an improvement in consistent condom use after a period of at least one year. This study showed that 58% of females visiting a health clinic for STDs one year after the CCU intervention reported CCU while the control group reported 45%. The other 49 studies either did not measure CCU (the best comparison with abstinent behavior), or did not find a significant program effect of at least one year. This pattern of evidence (1 success out of 49) does not provide a reasonable basis for replacing abstinence education with a condom-based sex education policy.

B. *Cross-contamination of Program Effects*: The benefits of a random assignment research design are best realized when the treatment and control group can be kept separate and their integrity can be maintained. In this way, the treatment or "medicine" is not shared between the groups. However, in field experiments, this requirement is difficult to achieve, especially with teenagers, and particularly with an intervention that deals with a topic as highly charged as sex. Students randomly assigned to the two groups don't live in these groups—they interact with friends, siblings, and dating partners in the other group. Any new values or behaviors adopted by each group are shared across the groups, and the longer that sharing lasts the more likely it is that the differences between the two groups will disappear as their attitudes, values, beliefs and behaviors merge over time. This cross-group contamination is likely to be a stronger intervention than a typical one-hour-per-day short-term intervention. With almost six years for this spillover effect to operate, this would minimize the measurable differences between the groups, even if the program had successfully reduced the participants' sexual activity. The Mathematica study did not address this problem, nor did it make exception for it in reporting its findings. This limitation and those that follow demonstrate that it requires more than an initial random assignment of participants to claim a "gold standard" study. It also illustrates how difficult it is to do good field studies.

C. *Non-Representative Study Sample*: The high-risk population used in the study does not represent the teen population in the U.S. (The majority of the sample were African American youth from poor, single-parent households.) The fact that these programs produced no impact on this sample does not indicate whether these same programs would have had an impact on a more representative group of teens.

D. *Unusually Long Follow-up Timeframe*: The follow-up time frame employed in this study—2 1/2 to 5 1/2 years after the program end—is too long for any type of sex education intervention to have a sustained effect on behavior without interim reinforcement of the program message. We are not aware of any evaluations of comprehensive sex education programs that have shown positive changes in teen condom use after three years, and are aware of only two that have shown impact after two years, and these were using the lower standard of success. A myriad of negative influences operate in adolescents' lives to overpower any initial program effect that may have occurred so far in the past. An outcome evaluation with a 5 1/2 year follow-up time period and no interim program reinforcement does not provide a realistic indication of program effectiveness.

E. *Inappropriate Timing of Program Dose*: The age group for the interventions in the Mathematica study was quite young—elementary and early middle school. Some were as young as 4th and 5th grade. The interventions did not continue, follow-up with, or reinforce the initial treatment during the key years (9th, 10th, 11th grade) when transition into sexual activity typically occurs. Thus, the treatment was not delivered or reinforced when it was most relevant and needed. As stated in the Mathematica report "the findings provide no information on the effects programs might have if they were implemented for high school youth or began at earlier ages but served youth through high school." At the outset then, the evaluation started with programs that had little hope of impacting behavior in the long run.

F. *Inadequate Utilization of Mediator Variables*: A major disappointment with the study was the insufficient attention given to identifying and tracking the important causal factors that mediate adolescent sexual risk behavior. The study's generic logic model was not tailored to the four specific programs, and therefore the specific theory of these programs was not tested. Without understanding and monitoring these causal factors, success or failure cannot be understood or explained, intervention modifications can not be made, and longer term program potential cannot be identified. Of the mediating variables they did measure and test, only two showed a significant relationship to the targeted behavior, but neither of them showed significant pre–post change. A more appropriate evaluation model for new and developing programs is one that would share interim data with programs to support their evolution and improvement. In Mathematica's case, data was not shared with the programs until four or five years later. Had we taken that approach with some of our own program evaluations, (e.g., Arkansas, Virginia, South Carolina, Georgia) we would likely have seen the same result when measuring behavior five years later. Instead, these projects have evolved and matured over time, and are now realizing up to 50% reduction in initiation of sexual activity.

V. Evidence of Abstinence Effectiveness

Several well designed evaluations of abstinence programs have found significant, long-term reductions in adolescent sexual activity, with both moderate and high-risk populations.

A. A randomized controlled trial conducted by [social science researcher John] Jemmott et al. found that an abstinence-only intervention significantly reduced sexual initiation among young African American adolescents after a 24-month follow-up period, and did not reduce condom use for those virgins who did become sexually active.

B. An abstinence curriculum that was taught in addition to an existing comprehensive sex education program decreased sexual initiation by approximately 40% after 20 months for program students versus comparison students in a high-risk population.

C. An evaluation of the *Reasons of the Heart* abstinence curriculum found that adolescent program participants were approximately one half as likely as the matched comparison group to initiate sexual activity after one year. The program's effect was as strong for the African American subgroup in the sample as it was overall.

D. A study of the *Heritage Keepers* abstinence program found that one year after program participation virgin middle school students were about one half as likely to initiate sexual activity as the comparison group. Roughly one half of the sample was African American, for whom the program effect was equally strong.

E. The *Sex Respect and Teen Aid* abstinence-only programs reduced the rate of initiation of sex by more than one third for the high-risk students in a Caucasian high school sample after 12 months.

Abstinence education addresses the relationship of sexuality to the well-being of the whole person.

VI. Benefits of Abstinence

Abstinence education offers benefits to adolescents and society that are not found in the comprehensive sex education approach.

A. Abstinence provides 100% protection from the biological consequences of sex (pregnancy, abortion, teen parenthood, the full spectrum of STDs).

B. Youth who abstain can avoid the negative emotional consequences related to teen sex—lowered self-esteem, regret, depression, etc.—as well as reducing the likelihood of experiencing sexual coercion and sexual violence.

C. Abstinence programs emphasize principles of self-restraint, self-esteem, future goals, long-term commitment, and unselfishness in relationships, and teach healthy relationship skills, all of which support the formation of strong marriages and healthy families.

D. Several studies have found that teaching abstinence does not reduce rates of condom use for virgin teens who become sexually active.

E. Abstinence education addresses the relationship of sexuality to the well-being of the whole person, rather than treating sexual activity as an isolated and unrelated behavior.

VII. Programs That Work

Our research shows, not surprisingly, that some programs work and some don't. The important questions are "which ones do, and why?" Abstinence interventions are most effective if they incorporate what has been learned about how to reduce adolescent sexual risk behavior.

A. Well designed programs target teen attitudes, values, efficacy, and goals regarding abstinence, sexuality, and relationships, as key mediators of sexual behavior.

B. The classroom teacher plays a crucial role in the process of changing teen attitudes and behaviors about sexuality through his/her personal example, mentoring, and teaching skills.

C. Successful programs utilize a variety of instructional methods that include interactive participatory activities, role playing, skill-building, personal application, and commitment.

D. An initial program installment of 20 hours of instruction, repeated annually, and followed by regular reinforcement of the abstinence message is the minimum dose recommended to facilitate an increase in teen sexual abstinence.

E. Well designed abstinence interventions will contain a strong parent component that includes direct parent instruction and "homework" assignments to facilitate parent-teen interaction about abstinence.

Well designed and well implemented abstinence education programs can reduce teen sexual activity by as much as one half for periods of one to two years, substantially increasing the number of adolescents who avoid the full range of problems related to teen sexual activity. Abandoning this strategy because of one study containing numerous limitations and shifting to a strategy that has shown little success across a broad range of studies, would appear to be a policy driven by politics rather than by a desire to protect American teens.

6

Abstinence-Only Programs Do Not Delay Teen Sex

Mathematica Policy Research, Inc.

Mathematica Policy Research, Inc. endeavors to provide high-quality, objective research for society's most pressing issues. Their recent reports have focused on teacher certification, healthcare costs, and welfare programs.

After investigating four abstinence-only programs from across the nation, it is clear that such programs have no impact on when or whether teens will engage in sexual intercourse. Program group members were no more likely than control group members to have abstained from sex, including unprotected sex. In addition, participants in both groups began having sex at around the same age and had around the same number of sex partners. Given these findings, it is important that young people receive accurate information about sex throughout their adolescence and that peer group support be encouraged.

The enactment of Title V, Section 510 of the Personal Responsibility and Work Opportunity Reconciliation Act of 1996 significantly increased the funding and prominence of abstinence education as an approach to promote sexual abstinence and healthy teen behavior. Since fiscal year 1998, the Title V, Section 510 program has allocated $50 million annually in federal funding for programs that teach abstinence from sexual activity outside of marriage as the expected stan-

Christopher Trenholm and Barbara Devaney, "Impacts of Four Title V, Section 510 Abstinence Education Programs," Princeton, NJ: Mathematica Policy Research, Inc., 2007. © 2007 Mathematica Policy Research, Inc. Reproduced by permission.

dard for school-age children. Under the matching block grant program administered by the U.S. Department of Health and Human Services (DHHS), states must match this federal funding at 75 percent, resulting in a total of $87.5 million annually for Title V, Section 510 abstinence education programs. All programs receiving Title V, Section 510 abstinence education funding must comply with the "A-H" definition of abstinence education.

In the Balanced Budget Act of 1997, Congress authorized a scientific evaluation of the Title V, Section 510 Abstinence Education Program. This report presents final results from a multi-year, experimentally based impact study conducted as part of this evaluation. It focuses on four selected Title V, Section 510 abstinence education programs: (1) *My Choice, My Future!* in Powhatan, Virginia; (2) *ReCapturing the Vision* in Miami, Florida; (3) *Families United to Prevent Teen Pregnancy (FUPTP)* in Milwaukee, Wisconsin; and (4) *Teens in Control* in Clarksdale, Mississippi. Based on follow-up data collected from youth four to six years after study enrollment, the report presents the estimated program impacts on youth behavior, including sexual abstinence, risks of pregnancy and sexually transmitted diseases (STDs), and other related outcomes.

Program Specifics

The four selected programs offered a range of implementation settings and program strategies, reflecting the array of operational experiences of the Title V, Section 510 programs operating nationwide. The programs served youth living in a mix of urban communities (Miami and Milwaukee) and rural areas (Powhatan, Virginia and Clarksdale, Mississippi). In three of these communities, the youth served were predominantly African-American or Hispanic and from poor, single-parent households. In Powhatan, youth in the programs were mostly white, non-Hispanic youth from working- and middle-class, two-parent households.

Other key dimensions of program variation include the following:

- Program Delivery. The four programs differed substantially in their setting, program type, and attendance requirements.

  - Setting: Although all four programs served youth in school settings, *FUPTP* served youth after school and the other three programs served youth in classrooms during the school day much like any other course.

  - Program Type: Two of the programs were offered on an elective basis (*ReCapturing the Vision* and *FUPTP*), while the other two programs were nonelective classes.

  - Attendance: One program had voluntary attendance (*FUPTP*); the other three had mandatory attendance.

- Ages of Youth Served. Two of the programs—*My Choice, My Future!* and *ReCapturing the Vision*—targeted youth in middle school grades, while the other two programs targeted youth in upper elementary grades.

- Program Duration and Intensity. Although all programs offered more than 50 contact hours, making them relatively intense among programs funded by the Title V, Section 510 grant, two of the programs—*ReCapturing the Vision* and *FUPTP*—were particularly intensive. These two programs met every day of the school year and youth could participate in *FUPTP* for up to four years.

- Other Services Available to Youth. Two of the programs—*ReCapturing the Vision* and *FUPTP*—operated in communities with a rich set of health, family life, and sex education services available through the public schools, while the remaining two programs operated in schools with limited services as part of their existing school curricula.

Evaluation Design

In response to the Congressional authorization of a scientific evaluation of the Title V, Section 510 Abstinence Education Program, the evaluation used an experimental design. Under this design, eligible youth were randomly assigned to either the program group, which was offered Title V, Section 510 abstinence education program services, or the control group that was not offered these services. The rigor of the experimental design derives from the fact that, with random assignment, youth in both the program and control groups were similar in all respects except for their access to the abstinence education program services. As a result, differences in outcomes between the program and control groups could be attributed to the abstinence education program and not to any pre-existing unobserved differences between the program and control groups.

Findings indicate that youth in the program group were no more likely than control group youth to have abstained from sex.

This report is based on a final follow-up survey administered to 2,057 youth; just less than 60 percent (1,209) were assigned to the program group; the remainder (848) were assigned to the control group. The survey was administered to youth in 2005 and early 2006—roughly four to six years after they began participating in the study. By this time, youth in the study sample had all completed their programs, in some cases several years earlier, and averaged about 16.5 years of age. Across the programs, the mean age was higher (roughly 18 years of age) for study youth in the two middle school programs, *ReCapturing the Vision* and *My Choice, My Future!*, while it was lower (around 15 years of age) for those in the two upper elementary school programs, *FUPTP* and *Teens in Control*.

The impact evaluation draws on a rich longitudinal data set that includes measures of sexual abstinence and teen risk behavior, knowledge of the consequences of sexual activity, and perceptions about the risks of pregnancy and STDs. Two main sets of outcome measures were constructed from the follow-up survey data:

1. Sexual Behavior. Rates of sexual abstinence, rates of unprotected sex, number of sexual partners, expectations to abstain, and reported rates of pregnancy, births, and STDs.

2. Knowledge and Perceptions of Risks Associated with Teen Sexual Activity. Scale measures of STD identification (from among a list of diseases), risks of pregnancy and STDs from unprotected sex, and health consequences of STDs; youth perceptions of the effectiveness of condoms and birth control pills for pregnancy prevention and for the prevention of several types of STDs, including HIV, chlamydia and gonorrhea, and herpes and human papillomavirus (HPV).

Impacts on Behavior

Findings indicate that youth in the program group were no more likely than control group youth to have abstained from sex and, among those who reported having had sex, they had similar numbers of sexual partners and had initiated sex at the same mean age. Contrary to concerns raised by some critics of the Title V, Section 510 abstinence funding, however, program group youth were no more likely to have engaged in unprotected sex than control group youth. Specific findings follow.

Sexual Abstinence. Program and control group youth were equally likely to have remained abstinent. About half of both groups of youth reported remaining sexually abstinent, and a slightly higher proportion reported having been abstinent within the 12 months prior to the final follow-up survey (56 percent of program group youth versus 55 percent of control group youth; this difference was not statistically significant).

Unprotected Sex. Program and control group youth did not differ in their rates of unprotected sex, either at first intercourse or over the last 12 months. Over the last 12 months, 23 percent of both groups reported having had sex and always using a condom; 17 percent of both groups reported having had sex and only sometimes using a condom; and 4 percent of both groups reported having had sex and never using a condom.

Age at First Intercourse. For both the program and control group youth, the reported mean age at first intercourse was identical, 14.9 years. This age is seemingly young, but recall that the outcome is defined only for youth who reported having had sex and the average age of the evaluation sample was less than 17.

Sexual Partners. Program and control group youth also did not differ in the number of partners with whom they had sex. Comparing the program and control groups overall, the distributions on the number of reported sex partners are nearly identical. About one-quarter of all youth in both groups had sex with three or more partners, and about one in six had sex with four or more partners.

Impacts on Knowledge of Risks Associated with Teen Sex

Overall, the programs improved identification of STDs but had no overall impact on knowledge of unprotected sex risks and the consequences of STDs. Both program and control group youth had a good understanding of the risks of pregnancy but a less clear understanding of STDs and their health consequences.

STD Identification. On the follow-up survey, youth were given a list of 13 diseases and asked whether or not each was a sexually transmitted disease; nine were actual STDs and four were not STDs. Youth in the program group identified an average of 69 percent of these diseases correctly. This rate is two percentage points higher than the average among youth in the control group, and the difference is statistically significant.

Study youth are less knowledgeable about the potential health risks from STDs.

Findings remain consistent when examining impacts separately for diseases that are STDs and those that are not. This consistency suggests that programs did not simply raise the likelihood that youth believed any disease was transmitted sexually; rather, they had a beneficial long-term impact on STD identification.

Knowledge of Unprotected Sex Risks. Most youth are knowledgeable about the risks of unprotected sex. On a two-item [0–1] scale measuring knowledge of these risks, youth in both the program and control group reported a high mean score (0.88).

Knowledge of STD Consequences. In contrast to high levels of knowledge about the risks of unprotected sex, study youth are less knowledgeable about the potential health risks from STDs. On a three-item [0–1] scale measuring their understanding of these risks, youth in the program and control groups had nearly identical mean scores of 0.52 and 0.51, respectively, which corresponded to a typical youth answering only about half the items of the scale correctly.

Impacts on Perceptions of Pregnancy and STD Prevention

Perceived Effectiveness of Condoms. Program and control group youth had similar perceptions about the effectiveness of condoms for pregnancy prevention. About half of the youth in both groups reported that condoms usually prevent pregnancy, and 38 percent reported that condoms sometimes prevent pregnancy. Only three percent of youth reported that condoms never prevent pregnancy, while seven percent reported being unsure.

With respect to STD prevention, a number of youth in both the program and control groups reported being unsure about the effectiveness of condoms at preventing STDs. For example, roughly one-quarter of youth in both groups reported being unsure about whether condoms are effective at preventing chlamydia and gonorrhea or at preventing herpes and HPV. In addition, a sizeable fraction in both groups, about one-in-seven, reported being unsure about condoms' effectiveness for preventing HIV. These findings are in sharp contrast to those for pregnancy, for which very few youth in either group reported being unsure about their effectiveness.

Program group youth were less likely than control group youth to report that condoms are usually effective at preventing STDs; and they were more likely to report that condoms are never effective at preventing STDs. For example, 21 percent of program group youth reported that condoms never prevent HIV, compared to 17 percent of control group youth. For herpes and HPV, 23 percent of program group youth reported that condoms are never effective, compared to 15 percent of control group youth.

Perceived Effectiveness of Birth Control Pills. Just over 55 percent of the youth in both the program and control groups reported that, when used properly, birth control pills usually prevent pregnancy. With respect to STD prevention, more than two out of three youth reported, correctly, that birth control pills do not prevent STDs. And, for each type of STD investigated, a significantly higher proportion of youth in the program group than in the control group reported this was the case. For example, 73 percent of program group youth correctly reported that birth control pills never prevent HIV compared to 69 percent of control group youth, a statistically significant difference of four points. . . .

Looking Forward

The evaluation highlights the challenges faced by programs aiming to reduce adolescent sexual activity and its consequences. Nationally, rates of teen sexual activity have declined over the past 15 years, yet even so, about half of all high school youth report having had sex, and more than one in five report having had four or more partners by the time they graduate from high school. One-quarter of sexually active adolescents nationwide have an STD, and many STDs are life-long viral infections with no cure.

Findings . . . provide no evidence that abstinence programs implemented in upper elementary and middle schools are effective in reducing the rate of teen sexual activity.

Some policymakers and health educators have questioned whether the Title V, Section 510 programs' focus on abstinence elevates these STD risks. Findings from this study suggest that this is not the case, as program group youth are no more likely to engage in unprotected sex than their control group counterparts. However, given the lack of program impacts on behavior, policymakers should consider two important factors as they search for effective ways to reduce the high rate of teen sexual activity and its negative consequences:

Targeting youth solely at young ages may not be sufficient. As with the four programs in this study, most Title V, Section 510 abstinence education programs were implemented in upper elementary and middle schools. In addition, most Title V, Section 510 programs are completed before youth enter high school, when rates of sexual activity increase and many teens are either contemplating or having sex.

Findings from this study provide no evidence that abstinence programs implemented in upper elementary and middle schools are effective in reducing the rate of teen sexual activity. However, the findings provide no information on the effects programs might have if they were implemented for high school youth or began at earlier ages but continued to serve youth through high school.

Peer support may be protective but erodes sharply during the teen years. An analysis of teen sexual activity ... finds that friends' support for abstinence is a significant predictor of future sexual abstinence. Although the programs had at most a small impact on this measure in the short-term and no impact in the longer-term, this finding suggests that promoting support for abstinence among peer networks should be an important feature of future abstinence programs.

While friends' support for abstinence may have protective benefits, maintaining this support appears difficult for most youth as they move through adolescence. At the time when most Title V, Section 510 abstinence education programs are completed and youth enter their adolescent years, data from the study find that support for abstinence among friends drops dramatically. For example, survey data from the start of the impact study show that nearly all youth had friends who exhibited attitudes and behaviors supportive of abstinence. Four years later, however, the typical youth in the study reported that only two of his or her five closest friends remained supportive of abstinence.

Youth who participate in Title V, Section 510 programs may also find themselves unable to maintain their peer networks as they advance from elementary to middle school or from middle school up through high school. In some urban settings, for example, the parent(s) of a child attending a particular middle school might have the option of sending that child to potentially dozens of high schools in the school district. Alternatively, in many other communities, children from several elementary (or middle) schools might feed into a single middle (or high) school. To the extent that the Title V, Section 510 abstinence programs aim to influence peer networks, this dispersal or dilution of peer networks after youth complete the programs presents a significant challenge to sustaining positive change.

7

Comprehensive Sex Education Does Not Delay Teen Sex

The Administration for Children and Families and Department of Health and Human Services

The Administration for Children and Families (ACF), within the Department of Health and Human Services (HHS), is responsible for federal programs that promote the economic and social well-being of families, children, individuals, and communities.

A review of nine of the most commonly used comprehensive sex education (CSE) programs reveals that they have little impact on teens' decisions to delay sexual intercourse. Although these programs demonstrate a small impact on increasing the use of condoms among adolescents, the positive effects lessen over time. While the literature used in these programs is largely medically accurate, more attention needs to be paid to condom failure rates.

"Comprehensive Sex Education" curricula for adolescents have been endorsed by various governmental agencies, educational organizations, and teenage advocacy groups as the most effective educational method for reducing teenage pregnancy and helping prevent the spread of sexually transmitted diseases (STDs) among America's youth. The National Institutes of Health (NIH) defines Comprehensive Sex Education (CSE) as "teaching both abstinence and the use of protective methods for sexually active youth"; NIH states that CSE cur-

The Administration for Children and Families (ACF) and Department of Health and Human Services (HHS), "Review of Comprehensive Sex Education Curricula," May 2007.

ricula have been "shown to delay sexual activity among teens." Non-governmental groups that support CSE have also made statements linking CSE curricula to abstinence as well as reduction of pregnancy and sexually transmitted infections (STIs).

The Administration for Children and Families, within the Department of Health and Human Services undertook an examination of some of the most common CSE curricula currently in use. The purpose of this examination was to inform federal policymakers of the content, medical accuracy, and effectiveness of CSE curricula currently in use.

In 2005, [US] Senators [Rick] Santorum and [Tom] Coburn requested that the Administration for Children and Families (ACF) review and evaluate comprehensive sex education programs supported with federal dollars. The Senators wrote to the Assistant Secretary for Children and Families,

> In particular, we would appreciate a review that explores the effectiveness of these programs in reducing teen pregnancy rates and the transmission of sexually transmitted diseases. In addition, please assess the effectiveness of these programs in advancing the greater goal of encouraging teens to make the healthy decision to delay sexual activity. Please also include an evaluation of the scientific accuracy of the content of these programs. Finally, we would appreciate an assessment of how the actual content of these programs compares to their stated goals.

In response, ACF contracted with the Sagamore Institute for Policy Research to review some of the most common CSE curricula currently in use. ACF also requested and received comments on these reviews from the Medical Institute for Sexual Health (MISH).

Research Questions and Methodology

In response to the request from Senators Santorum and Coburn, the curriculum reviews evaluated four questions:

1. Does the content of the comprehensive sex education curricula mirror the stated purposes?

2. What is the content of comprehensive sex education curricula?

3. Do comprehensive sex education curricula contain medically inaccurate statements?

4. Do evaluations of these curricula show them to be effective at (a) delaying sexual debut and (b) reducing sex without condoms?

The initial charge of this project was to evaluate the content and effectiveness of the "most frequently used" CSE curricula. After a thorough search, which included contacting publishers, researchers, distributors, and advocacy groups, it was determined that a list ranked by "frequency of use" or "number of copies purchased" was not in existence nor could one be produced.

Instead, curricula were chosen for this study based on the frequency and strength of endorsement received from leading and recognized sexuality information organizations and resources. A curriculum was considered to be "endorsed" if a source recommended it or promoted it as a "program that works." The curricula mentioned most frequently were chosen for this study if they were school-based (i.e. not solely for community organizations), widely available, and described by at least one source as "comprehensive" or "abstinence-plus." Additional weight was given to curricula described as evidence-based or as a "program that works."

It should be noted that some of the curricula reviewed do not state in their materials that they have an abstinence focus—i.e. that they are "comprehensive sex education," "abstinence plus," or in some other way focused on abstinence. However, if a curriculum were endorsed as "comprehensive" or "abstinence plus" by a leading sexuality information organization and resources, it was assumed that the curriculum would be purchased and used for the purpose of providing comprehensive sex education. Additionally of note, some of the curricula have recently published revisions with added abstinence components. In every case, the most recent version of the curricula available was studied.

Nine curricula met the criteria for this study and were subsequently reviewed:

1. *Reducing the Risk: Building Skills to Prevent Pregnancy, STD & HIV (4th Edition.)*, by R. Barth, 2004.

2. *Be Proud! Be Responsible!*, L. Jemmott, J. Jemmott, K. McCaffree, published by Select Media, Inc. 2003.

3. *Safer Choices: Preventing HIV, Other STD and Pregnancy (Level 1)*, by J. Fetro, R. Barth and K. Coyle, published by ETR Associates, 1998; and *Safer Choices: Preventing HIV, Other STD and Pregnancy (Level 2)*, by K. Coyle and J. Fetro, published by ETR Associates, 1998.

4. *AIDS Prevention for Adolescents in School*, by S. Kasen and I. Tropp, distributed by the Program Archive on Sexuality, Health, and Adolescence (PASHA), 2003.

5. *BART=Becoming a Responsible Teen (Revised Edition)*, by J. Lawrence, published by ETR (Education, Training, Research) Associates, 2005.

6. *Teen Talk: An Adolescent Pregnancy Prevention Program*, by M. Eisen, A. McAlister and G. Zellman, distributed by PASHA, 2003.

7. *Reach for Health, Curriculum, Grade 8*, by L. O'Donnell, et al., by Education Development Center, Inc., 2003.

8. *Making Proud Choices* by L. Jemmott, J. Jemmott, K. McCaffree, published by Select Media, Inc., 2001, 2002.

9. *Positive Images: Teaching Abstinence, Contraception, and Sexual Health*, by P. Brick and B. Taverner, published by Planned Parenthood of Greater Northern New Jersey, Inc., 2001.

The curriculum review consisted of four components. First, each curriculum underwent an extensive content analysis, i.e. a word-by-word count of instances in which certain words or themes (e.g. condoms, abstinence) are mentioned. Content analyses offer insight into the weight-respective curricula give to key themes. . . .

These curricula often do not spend as much time discussing abstinence as they do discussing contraception and ways to lessen risks of sexual activity.

Second, the stated purposes of the curricula were compared to the actual emphases of the curricula, as demonstrated by the content analysis.

Third, curriculum content was evaluated for medical accuracy, primarily the accuracy of statements about condoms (including statements on a common spermicide, nonoxynol-9, that was previously recommended to be added to condoms).

Lastly, evaluations of each curriculum—which offer insights into curriculum effectiveness at delaying sexual debut and increasing condom use—were located and summarized. . . .

Study Findings

The curriculum reviews yielded the following findings:

Does the content of the curricula mirror their stated purposes?
While the content of the curricula reviewed adheres to their stated purposes for the most part, these curricula often do not spend as much time discussing abstinence as they do discussing contraception and ways to lessen risks of sexual activity. Of the curricula reviewed, the curriculum with the most balanced discussion of abstinence and safer-sex still discussed condoms and contraception nearly seven times more than abstinence. Three of the nine curricula reviewed did not have a

stated purpose of promoting abstinence; however, two of these three curricula still discussed abstinence as an option (although, again, discussion of condoms and safer sex predominated). As a last note, it is important to recognize that, although some of the curricula do not include abstinence as a stated purpose, some sexuality information organizations and resources recommend these curricula as comprehensive sex education.

What is the content of comprehensive sex education curricula? As mentioned in the previous paragraph, these curricula focus on contraception and ways to lessen risks of sexual activity, although abstinence is at times a non-trivial component. Curriculum approaches to discussing contraception and ways to lessen risks of sexual activity can be grouped in three broad areas: (1) how to obtain protective devices (e.g. condoms), (2) how to broach a discussion on introducing these devices in a relationship, and (3) how to correctly use the devices. Below are a few excerpts from the curricula in these three areas.

- How to obtain protective devices: "How can you minimize your embarrassment when buying condoms? . . . Take a friend along; find stores where you don't have to ask for condoms (e.g. stocked on open counter or shelf); wear shades or a disguise so no one will recognize you; have a friend or sibling who isn't embarrassed buy them for you; make up a condom request card that you can hand to the store clerk (Show example)" (*AIDS Prevention for Adolescents in School*, p. 63).

- How to broach a discussion on introducing these devices in a relationship: "Teacher states: 'Pretend I am your sexual partner. I am going to read more excuses (for not using condoms) and I want you to convince me to use a condom'" (*Making Proud Choices*, p. 157).

- How to correctly use the devices: "Have volunteers come to the front of the room (preferably an equal number of males and females). Distribute one card to each. Give them a few minutes to arrange themselves in the proper order so their cards illustrate effective condom use from start to finish. Non-participants observe how the group completes this task and review the final order. When the order is correct, post the cards in the front of the room. CORRECT ORDER: (Sexual Arousal, Erection, Leave Room at the Tip, Roll Condom On, Intercourse, Orgasm/Ejaculation, Hold Onto Rim, Withdraw the Penis, Loss of Erection, Relaxation). Ask a volunteer to describe each step in condom use, using the index and middle finger or a model of a penis".

Do the curricula contain medically inaccurate statements?

Most comprehensive sex education curricula reviewed contain some level of medical inaccuracy. Of the nine curricula reviewed, three had no medically inaccurate statements. The most common type of medical inaccuracy involved promotion of nonoxynol-9, a common spermicide; three curricula had medical inaccuracies involving nonoxynol-9. While condoms with nonoxynol-9 (N-9) had previously been recommended for reducing the risk of HIV and other STDs in the 1990s, research over the last decade has demonstrated that nonxynol-9 is at best ineffective against STDs and HIV, and at worse increases risk.

Other inaccuracies included: (a) one curriculum that used the term "dental dam" instead of the FDA-approved "rubber dam", (b) one curriculum that quoted first year condom failure rates for pregnancy at 12%, when the correct statistic is 15%, and (c) one curriculum that stated that all condoms marketed in the United States "meet federal assurance standards" (which is not true).

In terms of inaccurate statistics related to condom effectiveness, eight of the nine curricula did not have any inaccuracies. The one curriculum which did have inaccuracies, *Making Proud Choices*, had three erroneous statements.

Although there were few inaccurate statements regarding condom effectiveness, the curricula do not state the risks of condom failure as extensively as is done in some abstinence-until-marriage curricula, nor do they discuss condom failure rates in context. Indeed, there were misleading statements in every curriculum reviewed. For example, one curriculum states, "When used correctly, latex condoms prevent pregnancy 97% of the time." While this statement is technically true, 15% percent of women using condoms for contraception experience an unintended pregnancy during the first year of "typical use," and 20% of adolescents under the age of 18 using condoms for contraception get pregnant within one year.

For perspective, it may be helpful to compare the error rate reported here with statistics cited in the December 2004 report entitled "The Content of Federally Funded Abstinence Education Programs," which is typically called the Waxman Report. This report found that, of thirteen abstinence-until-marriage curricula reviewed, eleven contained medically inaccurate statements; in all thirteen curricula (nearly 5,000 pages of information), there were 49 instances of questionable information. It could easily be argued that the comprehensive sex education curricula reviewed for this report have a similar rate of error compared with abstinence-until-marriage curricula.

Do evaluations of these curricula show them to be effective at (a) delaying sexual debut and (b) reducing sex without condoms? According to the evaluations reviewed, these curricula show some small positive impacts on (b) reducing sex without condoms, and to a lesser extent (a) delaying sexual debut. Specifically, there were evaluations for eight of the nine curricula reviewed. Of those eight curricula, seven showed at least some positive impacts on condom use; two showed some positive impacts on delay of sexual initiation. One curriculum

(*Teen Talk*) showed the only negative impact: for sexually in-experienced females, there was a negative impact on first intercourse and on consistent use of contraceptives. Often the impacts observed in evaluations are small, and most often the impacts do not extend three or six months after a curriculum has been used. It is important to note that evaluations of the curricula do have limitations. All curricula were evaluated by the curriculum authors themselves (although all evaluations were peer-reviewed and published in established journals). Also, the sample sizes are small in some of the evaluations, and research design issues decrease the ability to draw conclusions from some of the evaluations. . . .

Research on the effectiveness of nine commonly used comprehensive sex education curricula demonstrates that, while such curricula show small positive impacts on increasing condom use among youth, only a couple of curricula show impacts on delaying sexual debut; moreover, effects most often disappear over time. The fact that both the stated purposes and the actual content of these curricula emphasize ways to lessen risks associated with sexual activity—and not necessarily avoiding sexual activity—may explain why research shows them to be more effective at increasing condom use than at delaying sexual debut. Lastly, although the medical accuracy of comprehensive sex education curricula is nearly 100%—similar to that of abstinence-until-marriage curricula—efforts could be made to more extensively detail condom failure rates in context.

8

Abstinence-Only Education Prevents Teen Pregnancies

Paul Weyrich

The late Paul Weyrich was the co-founder of the Heritage Foundation, a conservative think tank that seeks to advance traditional American values through public policy reform.

Recent media attention has focused on the supposed failure of abstinence-only programs. Unfortunately, most of what has been reported has been biased towards a liberal agenda that supports teaching comprehensive sex education. Upon closer analysis, these reports and others that have been ignored reveal that abstinence-only education can prevent teen pregnancy and the transmission of sexually transmitted diseases (STDs).

Whoever coined the phrase "you can't argue with success" never ran into the folks who run the pro-abortion lobby. The representatives of these groups are willfully blind to the fact that more teens are open to the message of abstinence and to incorporating it into how they lead their lives. They realize that sexual activity without a binding commitment is a dead-end, the consequences ranging from hurt feelings at least to abortions, pregnancies, and sexually transmitted diseases. What should be common sense—no sex before marriage—is antithetical to the viewpoint of the staffs of organizations such as NARAL Pro-Choice America and The Alan Guttmacher Institute and their cheerleaders in the news media.

Paul Weyrich, "Abstinence Education Works," *Renew America*, February 15, 2005. Reproduced by permission of The Literary Estate of Paul Weyrich.

Most Teens Are Abstinent

The news media jumped upon a study by Texas A&M on the effectiveness of abstinence programs. News coverage about the report's findings indicated that children who received abstinence education were not working because teens were having sex after participating in abstinence education classes. However, the Associated Press did note that A&M researcher Buzz Pruitt "cautioned against drawing overarching conclusions from the study, which is incomplete and does have flaws" including the lack of a control group that would permit measurement of whether the increase in sexual activity would be even greater if teens had no abstinence education at all.

The Abstinence Clearinghouse examined the study by Texas A&M. It decided to compare results with those found by the Center for Disease Control's 2003 Youth Risk Behavior Surveillance survey. In essence, the Texas teens in the YRBS study became the control group. The finding? Abstinence Clearinghouse found that "When compared with the general teen population [in the 2003 YRBS survey], teens who participate in abstinence education programs have significantly lower sexual activity rates." The difference was most pronounced among young males. Only 24% of ninth grade males engaged in sexual activity after abstinence classes, nearly 20 percentage points less than those in the larger YRBS study. Nearly 40% of males in the 10th grade did engage in sexual activity, 17 percentage points less than those 10th grade teen males surveyed in the YRBS study.

When NBC polled young Americans recently about their feelings involving sex, the survey turned up some surprising results. Most teens 13–16 years old have not engaged in sexual intercourse. Many are concerned about the adverse consequences, which include pregnancy, sexually transmitted diseases, even their parents' reactions. Forty-two percent say they have not had sex because of their moral or religious beliefs. The findings speak to the good sense displayed by many young Americans.

If only some of their elders possessed such common sense. The entertainment industry constantly besieges teens with messages urging sex in its ceaseless production of movies, television programs and songs glorifying sex. Who wants to hear a song about "Because I had sex and picked up an STD, I will never have a child?"

The abstinence message can reach youth who are already sexually active.

Last fall, the RAND Institute released the results of a study conducted for the National Institute of Child Health and Development. It showed teens who watched shows with a great deal of sexual content were much more likely to engage in sexual intercourse than those teens who watched programs with little sexual content. "This is the strongest evidence yet that the sexual content of television programs encourages adolescents to initiate sexual intercourse and other sexual activities," stated RAND psychologist Rebecca Collins. It is with reason that my friend, Leslee Unruh, President of the Abstinence Clearinghouse, asserts "clean programming is essential" to encourage young Americans to hold positive attitudes toward sex. Hollywood evidently has a very different idea.

Rep. Henry Waxman (D-CA), Ranking Minority Member of the Committee on Government Reform, challenged the curriculums of abstinence programs, even faulting them for relying upon religious beliefs and moral values and for engaging in gender stereotyping. However, the report prepared by Waxman's own staff was shown to have engaged in faulty analysis. A lesson plan issued by Teen-Aid Inc. that he cited as having claimed as many as 15% of women would be unable to become pregnant after an abortion did not even include that statistic.

That lack of accurate information did not stop the pro-abortion lobby from welcoming the study. The response on their "Bush v. Choice" blog is likely to strike more than a few readers as being more suitable for scrawling on bathroom walls than to be placed on the webpage of a national lobbying organization. "Whatever it is that p—me off most, it seems that I'm not the only one," states the NARAL Pro-Choice America section on the Waxman report. ". . . abstinence-only programs also push bull—sex stereotypes." What specifically raises the ire of the writer? One point she takes exception to is, "One [abstinence-only] curriculum cited in the report teaches that women need 'financial support,' while men need admiration." Unless the young women who are pregnant come from a wealthy family, they generally do need financial support. Unfortunately, this assertion is just "not progressive" enough for the NARAL Pro-Choice America writer.

Effective Pro-Abstinence Programs

Conveniently ignored by the anti-abstinence forces are the good work of pro-abstinence programs such as Project Reality and Choosing the Best.

Project Reality's *Game Plan* program aimed at teens in grades seven to nine has been evaluated by Northwestern University researchers.

An August 2002 study by Northwestern University Medical School researcher John S. Lyons, Ph.D., discovered that "youth have a clearer understanding of abstinence and of the health consequences of engaging in or refraining from sexual activity after participating in the program. It also appears that the abstinence message can reach youth who are already sexually active. Finally, the reported behavioral intentions to remain abstinent from sexual activity until marriage increased significantly to two-thirds of all program participants."

The fact is that the best prevention against STDs and unplanned pregnancies is not having sex before marriage.

Lyons noted that there was a lack of a control group but added that the results would be unlikely to be achieved otherwise since most teens become more permissive about issues of sexual activity over time. The youth who were tested could simply be parroting back what their elders would like to hear. Even if that were so, Lyons said, ". . . that would be evidence that they clearly had heard the "Game Plan" message."

An October 8, 2004 executive summary prepared by Stan Weed, Ph.D., at the Department of Health & Human Services' Institute for Research and Development assessed the results for students in grades seven to nine in two Georgia counties, Pike and Spaulding. Of the 938 students, 549 received the Choosing the Best curricula while a comparison group of 389 students did not receive education. Spaulding was considered to be "higher risk" in regard to teen pregnancies. Pike was lower risk. Weed's research found that "Spaulding County experienced significant reductions in initiation rates in all three treatment grades compared to comparison students." The results were less clear for Pike County given the comparison groups. However, the overall finding made clear that teen sexual intercourse might be able to fall by between 50 to 60% when students were exposed to the curricula of "Choosing the Best" for three years.

More young Americans need to hear the abstinence message despite what the naysayers may say. The fact is that many teens seek sex not because they are happy and successful, but because the opposite is true. Catching an STD or experiencing an unplanned pregnancy is no self-esteem booster. The fact that the Center[s] for Disease Control and Prevention recently noted that America leads the developed world in deaths and disabilities related to STDs is no cause for celebration but good reason to take stock of where our country is headed. "Given the size and chronicity of HIV, HPV and other hepatitis virus epidemics, the overall health burden related to sexual behavior is unlikely to decline rapidly in the coming years," predicted the authors of the CDC study. With a gloomy finding like that, sensible Americans would think the opponents of abstinence would be willing to rethink their position.

The fact is that the best prevention against STDs and unplanned pregnancies is not having sex before marriage. . . .

9

Abstinence-Only Education Does Not Prevent Teen Pregnancies

Cynthia Dailard

The late Cynthia Dailard was a senior public policy associate at the Guttmacher Institute, a nonprofit group that provides information on sexual activity, contraception, abortion and childbearing.

Abstinence programs have been promoted by the United States government as the solution to reducing teen pregnancy and sexually transmitted diseases (STDs), but no evidence has shown that these programs are effective. In fact, it is difficult even to measure the effectiveness of these programs to know if they are working or failing. Many of the statistics that are used to support abstinence programs are flawed, such as comparing the perfect-use rate of abstinence with the typical-use rate of condoms, which is like comparing apples to oranges.

The word "sex" is commonly acknowledged to mean different things to different people. The same can be said for "abstinence." The varied and potentially conflicting meanings of "abstinence" have significant public health implications now that its promotion has emerged as the [George W.] Bush administration's primary answer to pregnancy and sexually transmitted disease (STD) prevention for all people who are not married.

Cynthia Dailard,"Understanding 'Abstinence': Implications for Individuals, Programs and Policies," *The Guttmacher Report on Public Policy*, December 2003, pp. 4–6. Reproduced by permission.

For those willing to probe beneath the surface, critical questions abound. What is abstinence in the first place, and what does it mean to use abstinence as a method of pregnancy or disease prevention? What constitutes abstinence "failure," and can abstinence failure rates be measured comparably to failure rates for other contraceptive methods? What specific behaviors are to be abstained from? And what is known about the effectiveness and potential "side effects" of programs that promote abstinence? Answering questions about what abstinence means at the individual and programmatic levels, and clarifying all of this for policymakers, remains a key challenge. Meeting that challenge should be regarded as a prerequisite for the development of sound and effective programs designed to protect Americans from unintended pregnancy and STDs, including HIV.

Common sense suggests that in the real world, abstinence as a contraceptive method can and does fail.

Abstinence and Individuals

What does it mean to use abstinence? When used conversationally, most people probably understand abstinence to mean refraining from sexual activity—or, more specifically, vaginal intercourse—for moral or religious reasons. But when it is promoted as a public health strategy to avoid unintended pregnancy or STDs, it takes on a different connotation. Indeed, President Bush has described abstinence as "the surest way, and the only completely effective way, to prevent unwanted pregnancies and sexually transmitted disease." So from a scientific perspective, what does it mean to abstain from sex, and how should the "use" of abstinence as a method of pregnancy of disease prevention be measured?

Population and public health researchers commonly classify people as contraceptive users if they or their partner are consciously using at least one method to avoid unintended pregnancy or STDs. From a scientific standpoint, a person would be an "abstinence user" if he or she intentionally refrained from sexual activity. Thus, the subgroup of people consciously using abstinence as a method of pregnancy or disease prevention is obviously much smaller than the group of people who are not having sex. The size of the population of abstinence users, however, has never been measured, as it has for other methods of contraception.

When does abstinence fail? The definition of an abstinence user also has implications for determining the effectiveness of abstinence as a method of contraception. The president, in his July 2002 remarks to South Carolina high school students, said, "Let me just be perfectly plain. If you're worried about teenage pregnancy, or if you're worried about sexually transmitted disease, abstinence works every single time." In doing so, he suggested that abstinence is 100% effective. But scientifically, is this in fact correct?

Researchers have two different ways of measuring the effectiveness of contraceptive methods. "Perfect use" measures the effectiveness when a contraceptive is used exactly according to clinical guidelines. In contrast, "typical use" measures how effective a method is for the average person who does not always use the method correctly or consistently. For example, women who use oral contraceptives perfectly will experience almost complete protection against pregnancy. However, in the real world, many women find it difficult to take a pill every single day, and pregnancies can and do occur to women who miss one or more pills during a cycle. Thus, while oral contraceptives have a perfect-use effectiveness rate of over 99%, their typical-use effectiveness is closer to 92%. As a result, eight in 100 women who use oral contraceptives will become pregnant in the first year of use.

Thus, when the president suggests that abstinence is 100% effective, he is implicitly citing its perfect-use rate—and indeed, abstinence is 100% effective if "used" with perfect consistency. But common sense suggests that in the real world, abstinence as a contraceptive method can and does fail. People who intend to remain abstinent may "slip" and have sex unexpectedly. Research is beginning to suggest how difficult abstinence can be to use consistently over time. For example, a recent study presented at the 2003 annual meeting of the American Psychological Society (APS) found that over 60% of college students who had pledged virginity during their middle or high school years had broken their vow to remain abstinent until marriage. What is not known is how many of these broken vows represent people consciously choosing to abandon abstinence and initiate sexual activity, and how many are simply typical-use abstinence failures.

Significant declines in U.S. teen pregnancy rates occurred prior to the implementation of government-funded programs supporting this particularly restrictive brand of abstinence-only education.

To promote abstinence, its proponents frequently cite the allegedly high failure rates of other contraceptive methods, particularly condoms. By contrasting the perfect use of abstinence with the typical use of other contraceptive methods, however, they are comparing apples to oranges. From a public health perspective, it is important both to subject abstinence to the same scientific standards that apply to other contraceptive methods and to make consistent comparisons across methods. However, researchers have never measured the typical-use effectiveness of abstinence. Therefore, it is not known how frequently abstinence fails in the real world or how effective it is compared with other contraceptive methods. This represents a serious knowledge gap. People deserve to have consistent and accurate information about the effectiveness of all contraceptive methods. For example, if they are told that abstinence is 100% effective, they should also be told that, if used correctly and consistently, condoms are 97% effective in preventing pregnancy. If they are told that condoms fail as much as 14% of the time, they should be given a comparable typical-use failure rate for abstinence.

What behaviors should be abstained from? A recent nationally representative survey conducted by the Kaiser Family Foundation and *Seventeen* magazine found that half of all 15–17-year-olds believed that a person who has oral sex is still a virgin. Even more striking, the APS study found that the majority (55%) of college students pledging virginity who said they had kept their vow reported having had oral sex. While the pledgers generally were somewhat less likely to have had vaginal sex than non-pledgers, they were equally likely to have had oral or anal sex. Because oral sex does not eliminate people's risk of HIV and other STDs, and because anal sex can heighten that risk, being technically abstinent may therefore still leave people vulnerable to disease. While the press is increasingly reporting that noncoital behaviors are on the rise among young people, no research data exists to confirm this.

Abstinence Education Programs

Defining and communicating what is meant by abstinence are not just academic exercises, but are crucial to public health efforts to reduce people's risk of pregnancy and STDs. For example, existing federal and state abstinence-promotion policies typically neglect to define those behaviors to be abstained from. The federal government will provide approximately $140 million in FY 2004 to fund education programs that exclusively promote "abstinence from sexual activity outside of marriage." The law, however, does not define "sexual activity." As a result, it may have the unintended effect of promoting noncoital behaviors that leave young people at risk. Currently, very little is known about the relationship between abstinence-promotion activities and the prevalence of noncoital activities.

This hampers the ability of health professionals and policy-makers to shape effective public health interventions designed to reduce people's risk.

Scarce public dollars could be better spent on programs that already have been proven to achieve delays in sexual activity of any duration, rather than on programs that stress abstinence until marriage.

There is no question, however, that increased abstinence—meaning delayed vaginal intercourse among young people—has played a role in reducing both teen pregnancy rates in the United States and HIV rates in at least one developing country. Research by The Alan Guttmacher Institute (AGI) indicates that 25% of the decrease in the U.S. teen pregnancy rate between 1988 and 1995 was due to a decline in the proportion of teenagers who had ever had sex (while 75% was due to improved contraceptive use among sexually active teens). A new AGI report also shows that declines in HIV-infection rates in Uganda were due to a combination of fewer Ugandans initiating sex at young ages, people having fewer sexual partners and increased condom use.

But abstinence proponents frequently cite both U.S. teen pregnancy declines and the Uganda example as "proof" that abstinence-only education programs, which exclude accurate and complete information about contraception, are effective; they argue that these programs should be expanded at home and exported overseas. Yet neither experience, in and of itself, says anything about the effectiveness of programmatic interventions. In fact, significant declines in U.S. teen pregnancy rates occurred prior to the implementation of government-funded programs supporting this particularly restrictive brand of abstinence-only education. Similarly, informed observers of the Ugandan experience indicate that abstinence-only education was not a significant program intervention during the years when Uganda's HIV prevalence rate was dropping. Thus, any assumptions about program effectiveness, and the effectiveness of abstinence-only education programs in particular, are misleading and potentially dangerous, but they are nonetheless shaping U.S. policy both here and abroad.

Accordingly, key questions arise about how to measure the success of abstinence-promotion programs. For example, the administration is defining program success for its abstinence-only education grants to community and faith-based organizations in terms of shaping young people's intentions and attitudes with regard to future sexual activity. In contrast, most public health experts stress the importance of achieving desired behavioral outcomes such as delayed sexual activity.

To date, however, no education program in this country focusing exclusively on abstinence has shown success in delaying sexual activity. Perhaps some will in the future. In the meantime, considerable scientific evidence already demonstrates that certain types of programs that include information about both abstinence and contraception help teens delay sexual activity, have fewer sexual partners and increase contraceptive use when they begin having sex. It is not clear what it is about these programs that leads teens to delay—a question that researchers need to explore. What is clear, however, is that no program of any kind has ever shown success in convincing young people to postpone sex from age 17, when they typically first have intercourse, until marriage, which typically occurs at age 25 for women and 27 for men. Nor is there any evidence that the "wait until marriage" message has any impact on young people's decisions regarding sexual activity. This suggests that scarce public dollars could be better spent on programs that already have been proven to achieve delays in sexual activity of any duration, rather than on programs that stress abstinence until marriage.

Finally, there is the question of whether delays in sexual activity might come at an unacceptable price. This is raised by research indicating that while some teens promising to abstain from sex until marriage delayed sexual activity by an average of 18 months, they were more likely to have unprotected sex when they broke their pledge than those who never pledged virginity in the first place. Thus, might strategies to promote abstinence inadvertently heighten the risks for people when they eventually become sexually active?

Difficult as it may be, answering these key questions regarding abstinence eventually will be necessary for the development of sound and effective programs and policies. At a minimum, the existing lack of common understanding hampers the ability of the public and policymakers to fully assess whether abstinence and abstinence education are viable and realistic public health and public policy approaches to reducing unintended pregnancies and HIV/STDs.

10

Sex Education Is More Effective Than Abstinence-Only Education

Simon Forrest

Simon Forrest is a London-based writer who focuses on social policy issues.

Educating young people is essential in combating the HIV/AIDS epidemic, but there is considerable debate about how best to deliver this information. Currently, no empirical evidence exists to support abstinence-only education in preventing HIV/AIDS, but political and moral agendas affect social policy and it remains the predominant method of sex education in the United States. Although abstinence remains the only sure way of preventing sexually transmitted diseases, comprehensive sex education can best give young people the knowledge they need to make safe choices during sexual activity.

Sex education is an important part of effective HIV prevention. It is generally accepted that it enables people to acquire knowledge and develop skills that they can use to protect and promote their sexual health through minimising the risks that they might face in the course of their sexual experiences. In recent years there has been discussion about what form sex education should take and the advantages and disadvantages of adopting an abstinence-based approach as an alternative to a more comprehensive approach. This discussion

Simon Forrest, "Abstinence Sex Education and HIV Prevention," AVERT, February 25, 2009. Reproduced by permission.

has assumed added significance with an increasing emphasis on the provision of funding for abstinence-based approaches to sex education in the United States and, now, through funds made available through PEPFAR (President's Emergency Plan For AIDS Relief), the prospect of advocates of abstinence-based approaches exporting their programmes of sex education to some of the parts of the world worst affected by HIV and AIDS. . . .

Abstinence-only vs. Comprehensive Sex Education

The main difference between abstinence-based and comprehensive approaches to sex education is that comprehensive approaches do not focus either solely or so closely on teaching young people that they should abstain from sex until they are married. And although they do explain to young people the potential benefits of delaying having sex until they are emotionally and physically ready, they also make sure that they are taught how to protect themselves from infections and pregnancy when they do decide to have sex. . . .

Despite the similarities in some of the things that supporters of abstinence-based and comprehensive approaches believe about sex education and what it can achieve in terms of young people's sexual health, it is probably overly optimistic to think that it is possible to build consensus on a single approach. This is because these superficial similarities mask profound differences in the values and attitudes which inform the views of supporters of abstinence-based and comprehensive sex education.

Many supporters of abstinence-based sex education have a background in or connection to Christian organisations that have strong views about sex and sexuality. Not only do they often believe that sex should only take place in the context of marriage, but some are also opposed to same-sex relationships and abortion. As a result of the strong faith basis for their beliefs about sex, supporters of abstinence education see the main objective as being to equip (and encourage) young people to refuse or avoid sex altogether, and they may exclude from their programmes any other information that they believe conflicts with this view. This may result in an abstinence-only course failing to include basic information about what activities transmit HIV and how such transmission can be avoided.

Even where supporters of abstinence-based sex education disavow a strong religious basis for their beliefs about what young people should be taught, they often highlight issues about fidelity to one partner, and reject provision of information about steps young people can take to protect themselves against disease and unintended pregnancy because they argue that to do so sends a mixed message.

Comprehensive sex education can reduce behaviors that put young people at risk of HIV, STIs and unintended pregnancy.

In contrast, most supporters of comprehensive sex education regard having sex and issues to do with sexuality as matters of personal choice that should not be dictated by religious or political dogmas. Working from an understanding of human rights, which means that people are entitled to access information about matters that affect them and the decisions that they make, they see sex education as being about providing young people with the means by which they can protect themselves against abuse and exploitation as well as unintended pregnancies, sexually transmitted diseases and HIV/ AIDS. They argue that without access to information about all aspects of sex and sexuality making these decisions freely is impossible. While they think that [it] is important that sex education is sensitive to faith issues, they assert that it should not be based on any set of specific religious values.

These fundamentally different views about sex and sexuality mean that supporters of abstinence-based and comprehensive approaches to sex education see the 'problem' of what to do about young people and sex quite differently and therefore reach quite different conclusions about the 'solution'. If, as supporters of comprehensive sex education tend to believe, the underlying premise of sexual health interventions is to meet social and utilitarian ideals then the solutions that are proposed are more likely to include earlier and more comprehensive sex education, more liberal abortion laws and freely available contraception. By contrast if, as supporters of abstinence-based approaches feel, the underlying motive has a strong religious dimension then the solutions are more likely to revolve around abstinence campaigns and be characterised by reluctance to promote contraception.

The Evidence Favors Comprehensive Sex Education

One of the ways in which the debate between supporters of abstinence and comprehensive approaches to sex education has been framed is in terms of which is the most effective.

Although at first glance the evidence can seem confusing, with claims coming from both groups about the proven effectiveness of programmes embodying their values, when only the most reliable studies are taken into account the position is clear. There is good evidence, from studies of programmes implemented in the US, UK and other European countries and countries in Africa and Asia, that comprehensive sex education can reduce behaviours that put young people at risk of HIV, STIs [sexually transmitted infections] and unintended pregnancy. Studies have repeatedly shown too that this kind of sex education does not lead to the earlier onset of sexual activity among young people and, in some cases, will even lead to it happening later.

In contrast there is no such robust evidence for the effectiveness of abstinence education. Almost all the studies that have claimed to show any positive outcomes are not well-enough designed to sustain these claims so it is not possible to infer whether they work or not from the research reports.

The research that is available currently shows at best mixed outcomes for abstinence-based approaches to sex education, benefiting some young people in the short term but placing them at greater risks later. For example, two studies suggest that for some young people making pledges to abstain from sexual intercourse until marriage does lead to delay in the timing of their first sexual intercourse. But these young people tend to hold strong religious beliefs and enjoy being an exclusive group among peers who do not take abstinence pledges. As the researchers note this means that pledging abstinence is not appropriate for young people who do not hold strong religious views and, moreover, if lots of young people are involved in making pledges (as using abstinence education as a method of sex education requires) the sense of being special will be dissipated. In addition, while an abstinence pledge may work for some groups of young people as a way of delaying when they have sexual intercourse, the majority still have sex before they are married and when they do they report using condoms less often than 'non-pledgers' and are more likely to substitute anal or oral sex for vaginal sexual intercourse. . . .

With regards to HIV prevention, a systematic review of all relevant studies, published in October 2007, concluded, "Evidence does not indicate that abstinence-only interventions effectively decrease or exacerbate HIV risk among participants in high-income countries; trials suggest that the programs are ineffective." Nevertheless the authors stressed the paucity of robust data and the need for more rigorous trials. They noted that most studies have been conducted among American youth, which may limit the generalisability of their findings.

Content Differences

Another way in which the debate gets framed is in relation to differences in beliefs about what the 'real facts' are that young people should be presented with in the context of sex education. Many supporters of abstinence-based sex education say that comprehensive programmes are too positive about the protective potential of contraceptives and understate their failure rate and the risks of contracting HIV or another STI. In addition, they criticise programmes of comprehensive sex education for placing too little emphasis on abstinence and sending young people a mixed message by referring both to abstaining from or delaying when they first have sexual intercourse, and the benefits of using contraception.

All the evidence clearly shows that the best way to progress HIV prevention through sex education is through comprehensive programmes.

For their part critics of abstinence-based programmes have said that they are too negative about the effectiveness of contraception and sometimes include inaccurate information about failure rates. Proponents of abstinence-based approaches have been accused of overstating condom failure rates, exaggerating the risks of infection with HIV and other STIs, reinforcing gender and sexuality stereotypes, and presenting sex and sexuality in an overly negative way.

The criticisms levelled against comprehensive programmes of sex education are difficult to sustain because research suggests that in practice many sex educators are very concerned not to present sex in too positive a light and tend to avoid coverage of sensitive and potentially embarrassing subjects like homosexuality and abortion. Young people consistently report that the underlying message is that they should not have sex. Moreover, much of the evidence for the ineffectiveness of condoms and other contraceptives cited by critics of comprehensive programmes is highly suspect, being based on poor quality research or the outcome of a partial reading of its results.

In contrast, those criticisms levelled at abstinence-based approaches do seem to have a firmer foundation. Some reviews of programme materials suggest factual inaccuracies— such as massively overestimating the prevalence of HIV and STIs and the failure rates of condoms when properly used— are common. These reviews have also shown that these programmes tend to project stereotypes about gender, repress information about positive aspects of sexual relationships, and overstate the emotional risks and dangers associated with sex. . . .

Importance for HIV/AIDS Prevention

Globally, the greatest HIV/AIDS burden falls on young people. Sex education is recognised as a major component of HIV prevention targeting young people; what form it takes and whether or not it works impacts directly on the HIV risk to which they are exposed. AIDS education for young people is a crucial factor in determining the extent to which they are at risk of HIV infection.

With the allocation of $15 billion under the President's Emergency Plan For AIDS Relief, abstinence education is being promoted in some of the countries worst affected by HIV and AIDS. This raises a number of concerns about whether this is an appropriate approach in contexts where HIV is very prevalent and sexual intercourse before marriage is widespread, and, particularly, whether such programmes will withhold accurate information about condoms.

All the evidence clearly shows that the best way to progress HIV prevention through sex education is through comprehensive programmes. Despite generating considerable debate and political support, particularly in the United States, abstinence education represents, primarily, a minority moral movement rather than an effective response to the sexual health needs and behaviour of young people.

As the experiences around the world demonstrate—a good example of which can be found in Uganda—what works in terms of sex education for HIV prevention is a comprehensive approach that is sensitive to the needs and experiences of particular groups. For unmarried, sexually active young people abstinence messages are not effective, whereas promoting faithfulness to one partner, condom use *and* abstinence is effective. Abstinence messages work to some extent for younger sexually inactive people, but they need to have information about contraception and risk-reduction behaviour for when they do decide to have sex. *Everyone* has the right to the information that can enable them to protect themselves against HIV infection—it is neither Christian nor moral to refuse them.

11

Abstinence-Only Education Is More Effective Than Sex Education

Douglas A. Sylva

Douglas A. Sylva is a Senior Fellow at the Catholic Family and Human Rights Institute (C-FAM). He researches and writes about public policy issues.

Teaching abstinence until marriage and fidelity within marriage has helped lower the rate of HIV/AIDS in Uganda. However, the international AIDS community continues to tout condoms as essential to stopping the spread of the disease, despite the lack of results in other African countries. The key to stopping the spread of HIV/AIDS in Africa is the embrace of traditional sexual morality and abstinence, as taught in Uganda.

As AIDS sweeps across Africa, Uganda remains a lone success story. Millions of Ugandans have embraced traditional sexual morality, including sexual abstinence outside of marriage and fidelity within marriage, in order to avoid infection. But the international AIDS community has been reluctant to promote this strategy elsewhere, continuing instead to place its faith in condoms.

According to a U.S. Agency for International Development (USAID) study of Uganda, "HIV prevalence peaked at around 15 percent in 1991, and had fallen to 5 percent as of 2001.

This dramatic decline in prevalence is unique worldwide." US-AID believes "the most important determinant of the reduction in HIV incidence in Uganda appears to be a decrease in multiple sexual partnerships and networks."

In comparison with other African nations, "Ugandan males in 1995 were less likely to have ever had sex . . . more likely to be married and keep sex within the marriage, and less likely to have multiple partners." USAID concludes that "the effect of HIV prevention in Uganda (particularly partner reduction) during the past decade appears to have had a similar impact as a potential medical vaccine of 80 percent efficacy. . . . A comprehensive behavior-change–based strategy . . . may be the most effective prevention approach."

Defending Condoms Despite the Evidence

However, the Ugandan experience is not being promoted elsewhere, which leads some observers to conclude that ideology may be playing a role. In fact, as news of the Ugandan success has spread, the defense of condoms has grown more insistent.

The international AIDS community appears determined to find a technological solution to the epidemic, rather than suggest the types of behavior change that have succeeded in Uganda.

Specifically, international AIDS activists have increased their attacks on the [George W.] Bush administration, which [sought] to incorporate abstinence training into the U.S. international AIDS program. Amy Coen, president of Population Action International, recently stated that "the importance of condoms cannot be overstated. Yet here in the United States, we are witnessing a retreat on the part of the government and a wall of silence descending around condom use. The case for condoms is indisputable." And, according to a column by Marie Cocco in Newsday, "President George W. Bush has begun appointing critics of condoms to a presidential advisory panel on AIDS. They include social conservatives who question the international scientific consensus that condoms are highly effective in AIDS prevention."

This promotion of condoms continues, despite the mounting evidence that they have failed to stem the spread of the disease. For instance, South Africa, led by Nelson Mandela, firmly has embraced the "safe-sex" strategy, and condom use has increased. But South Africa remains the world leader in AIDS infection, with 11.4 percent of its population currently infected.

The international AIDS community appears determined to find a technological solution to the epidemic, rather than suggest the types of behavior change that have succeeded in Uganda. The *Mercury News* of Miami recently reported that the Bill and Melinda Gates Foundation will spend $28 million to study the potential of birth-control diaphragms to combat AIDS in Africa. The *Mercury News* cautions, however, that "the scientific basis for diaphragms preventing AIDS is more theoretical than clinically proven."

Organizations to Contact

The editors have compiled the following list of organizations concerned with the issues debated in this book. The descriptions are derived from materials provided by the organizations. All have publications or information available for interested readers. The list was compiled on the date of publication of the present volume; the information provided here may change. Be aware that many organizations take several weeks or longer to respond to inquiries, so allow as much time as possible.

American Civil Liberties Union (ACLU)
915 15th Street NW, Washington, DC 20005
(202) 393-4930 • fax: (757) 563-1655
Web site: www.aclu.org

The ACLU is a national organization that works to defend Americans' civil rights as guaranteed by the U.S. Constitution. It opposes federal funding for abstinence-only sex education, arguing that it violates the civil rights and the freedom of speech of students and teachers. Among the ACLU's numerous publications are "Responsible Spending: Real Sex Ed for Real Lives," "Helping Teens Make Healthy and Responsible Decisions about Sex," and "Abstinence-Only Education Fact Sheet."

Alliance Defense Fund (ADF)
15100 N. 90th Street, Scottsdale, Arizona 85260
1-800-TELL-ADF • fax: (480) 444-0025
Web site: www.alliancedefensefund.org

The ADF is a legal alliance defending the right to hear and speak about Christian beliefs through the legal defense and advocacy of religious freedom, the sanctity of human life, and traditional family values. It believes that it is the responsibility of parents to educate their children about sex and defends the right of parents to remove their children from explicit sex education classes. In addition to position statements supporting these rights, the ADF Web site functions as a clearinghouse of news regarding sex education.

American Federation of Teachers (AFT)

555 New Jersey Ave. NW, Washington, DC 20001
(202) 879-4400
Web site: www.aft.org

The AFT, an affiliated international union of the AFL-CIO, was founded in 1916 to represent the economic, social, and professional interests of classroom teachers. It now includes paraprofessionals and school-related personnel; local, state and federal employees; higher education faculty and staff; and nurses and other healthcare professionals. The AFT supports comprehensive sex education and strongly argues against abstinence-only curricula as is expressed in their position statement, "Support for Reproductive Rights."

National Abstinence Education Association (NAEA)

1701 Pennsylvania Ave. NW, Suite 300
Washington, DC 2000
(202) 248-5420 • fax: (202) 580-6559
E-mail: info@abstinenceassociation.org
Web site: www.abstinenceassociation.org

Founded in 2006, the NAEA exists to serve, support, and represent individuals and organizations in the practice of abstinence education. As a non-profit organization, NAEA is able to offer unique member services for abstinence education organizations, educators, and providers, including unlimited lobbying on behalf of abstinence education. Among their many statements in support of abstinence-only education are "Abstinence Education Cuts Teen Sex by 50%" and "STD Crisis Requires Priority on Prevention."

National Association of State Boards of Education (NASBE)
277 South Washington Street, Suite 100
Alexandria, VA   22314
(703) 684-4000 • (703) 836-2313
E-mail: boards@nasbe.org
Web site: www.nasbe.org

A non-profit organization founded in 1958, NASBE works to strengthen state leadership in educational policy making, promote excellence in the education of all students, advocate equality of access to educational opportunity, and assure continued citizen support for public education. NASBE is opposed to abstinence-only education and endorses comprehensive sex education. In addition to providing a clearinghouse of the latest news reports concerning sex education, NASBE's Web site offers several position statements, including "Sex Education" and "Debate over Abstinence Education."

National Coalition Against Censorship (NCAC)
275 Seventh Ave., Suite 1504, New York, NY   10001
(212) 807-6222 • (212) 807-6245
E-mail: ncac@ncac.org
Web site: www.ncac.org

Founded in 1974, the NCAC is an alliance of 50 national non-profit organizations, including literary, artistic, religious, educational, professional, labor, and civil liberties groups. United by a conviction that freedom of thought, inquiry, and expression is a fundamental human right and essential to a healthy democracy, the NCAC works to educate its members and the public at large about the dangers of censorship and how to oppose them. As expressed in several position statements, including "Fighting Abstinence-Only Education," the NCAC argues that abstinence-only education violates student and teacher rights to freedom of speech.

National Education Association (NEA)
1201 16th Street NW, Washington, DC   20036-3290
(202) 833-4000 • fax: (202) 822-7974

Web site: www.nea.org

The NEA is an international, volunteer-based association of educators committed to advancing the cause of public education. The NEA argues that all students should have access to important health and sexuality information through appropriately established sex education programs in order to protect themselves and make informed decisions. Their Web site provides access to a number of position statements and research reports regarding sex education.

National Youth Advocacy Coalition (NYAC)
1638 R Street NW, Suite 300, Washington, DC   20009
800-541-6922 • fax: (877) 492-8916
E-mail: nyac@nyacyouth.org
Web site: www.nyacyouth.org

The NYAC is the leading national social justice and capacity-building organization working with lesbian, gay, bisexual, transgender and questioning (LGBTQ) youth and LGBTQ youth-serving professionals. The NYAC is opposed to abstinence-only education largely because it alienates gay and lesbian students and does not educate all youth about safe sex. In addition to several position statements regarding sex education, the NYAC also provides resources for educators and young people, including "You Know Different" and "New Infection Figures from the CDC Show Increase in HIV Highest Among Youth."

The Pro-Choice Public Education Project (PEP)
PO Box 3952, New York, NY   10163
(212) 977.4266
E-mail: pep@protectchoice.org
Web site: www.protectchoice.org

The PEP is dedicated to engaging young women about the critical issue of reproductive justice. The PEP is opposed to abstinence-only education and seeks to provide sex education that is comprehensive. In addition to many resources for educators and young people, the PEP Web site serves as clearinghouse for information regarding sex education and female sexuality.

Rethinking Schools
1001 E. Keefe Ave., Milwaukee, WI   53212
(414) 964-9646 • fax: (414) 964-7220
E-mail: fred.mckissack@gmail.com
Web site: www.rethinkingschools.org

Rethinking Schools began as a local effort in Milwaukee, Wisconsin to address problems such as basal readers, standardized testing, and textbook-dominated curricula. Since its founding in 1986, it has grown into a nationally prominent publisher of educational materials, with subscribers in all fifty states, all ten Canadian provinces, and many other countries. Rethinking Schools maintains an extensive collection of information regarding sex education, including articles such as "Let's Talk about Sex: Why Aren't We Telling Kids the Full Story?" and "Preaching Ain't Teaching: Sex Education and America's New Puritans."

Sexuality Information and Education Council of the United States (SIECUS)
90 John Street, Suite 704, New York, NY   10038
(212) 819-9770 • fax: (212) 819-9776
E-mail: pmalone@siecus.org
Web site: www.siecus.org

Founded in 1964, SIECUS provides education and information about sexuality and sexual and reproductive health. SIECUS advocates for the right of all people to have access to accurate information, comprehensive education about sexuality, and sexual health services. In addition to providing a sex education library on their main Web site, SIECUS also manages nomoremoney.org, a Web site dedicated to raising awareness about how to U.S. federal funding is being used to sponsor abstinence-only education.

Bibliography

Books

Michael J. Bradley *When Things Get Crazy With Your Teen: The Why, the How, and What to Do Now*. New York: McGraw-Hill, 2009.

Carolyn Cocca, ed. *Adolescent Sexuality: A Historical Handbook and Guide*. Westport, CT: Praeger, 2006.

Bruce Cook *Choosing the Best SOUL MATE: A Relationship and Abstinence Curriculum*. Atlanta: Choosing the Best Publishing, LLC, 2004.

Sean Covey *The Six Most Important Decisions You'll Ever Make: A Guide For Teens*. New York: Fireside, 2006.

Hayley DiMarco *Technical Virgin: How Far is Too Far?* Grand Rapids, MI: Revell, 2006.

Alesha E. Doan and Jean Calterone Williams *The Politics of Virginity: Abstinence in Sex Education*. Westport, CT: Praeger, 2008.

Dawn Eden *The Thrill of the Chaste: Finding Fulfillment While Keeping Your Clothes On*. Nashville, TN: W Publishing Group, 2006.

Nancy Ehrenreich, ed.	*The Reproductive Rights Reader: Law, Medicine, and the Construction of Motherhood.* New York: New York University Press, 2008.
Lakita Garth	*The Naked Truth.* Ventura, CA: Regal, 2007.
Rhett Godfrey	*The Teen Code: How to Talk to Us About Sex, Drugs, and Everything Else: Teenagers Reveal What Works Best.* Emmaus, PA: Rodale, 2004.
Edward C. Green	*The ABC Approach to Preventing the Sexual Transmission of HIV: Common Questions and Answers.* McLean, VA: Christian Connections for International Health, 2007.
Sandra Augustyn Lawton, ed.	*Sexual Health Information for Teens.* 2nd ed. Detroit, MI: Omnigraphics, 2008.
Mike Linderman	*The Teen Whisperer: How to Break Through the Silence and Secrecy of Teenage Life.* New York: Collins, 2007.
Eric and Leslie Ludy	*Teaching True Love to a Sex-at-13 Generation: The Ultimate Guide For Parents.* Nashville, TN: W Publishing Group, 2005.
Jamie L. Mullaney	*Everyone Is NOT Doing It: Abstinence and Personal Identity.* Chicago: University of Chicago Press, 2006.

Wendy Shalit

Girls Gone Mild: Young Women Reclaim Self-Respect and Find It's Not Bad to Be Good. New York: Random House, 2007.

Chandra Sparks Taylor

The Pledge. Washington, DC: Turnaround, 2008.

R. Murray Thomas

Sex and the American Teenager: Seeing Through the Myths and Confronting The Issues. Lanham, MD: Rowman and Littlefield Education, 2009.

Kris Vallotton

Purity: The New Moral Revolution. Shippensburg, PA: Destiny Image Publishing, 2008.

Sabrina Weill

The Real Truth About Teens and Sex: From Hooking Up to Friends With Benefits: What Teens are Thinking, Doing, and Talking About, and How to Help Them Make Smart Choices. New York: Perigee, 2005.

Youth Communication

Why I'm Still a Virgin: Teens Write About Saying No to Sex. New York, NY: 2007.

Periodicals

Jonathan Allen

"Abstinence Camp Just Says No," *CQ Weekly*, May 28, 2007.

American School Board Journal

"Kids Consider Abstinence-Only Sex Education a Suggestion," June 2007.

Nicholas Bakalar "Abstinence-Only Programs Not Found to Prevent H.I.V.," *New York Times*, August 14, 2007.

Elizabeth Bernstein "Sex-Ed Class Becomes Latest School Battleground," *Wall Street Journal*, March 30, 2006.

Mary C. Breaden "Impact of Sex Education On Pregnancy Examined," *Education Week*, April 2, 2008.

Heidi Bruggink "Abstinence-Only Funding (Finally) Set to Expire—But Don't Applaud Quite Yet," *Humanist*, July/August 2007.

Christian Century "Democrats to Cut Off Abstinence-Only Funds," June 12, 2007.

Christian Science Monitor "Honesty About Abstinence-Only," April 24, 2007.

Jonathan Cohen and Tony Tate "The Less They Know, the Better: Abstinence-Only HIV/AIDS Programs in Uganda," *Reproductive Health Matters*, November 2006.

Economist "Just Say No," February 14, 2009.

Jessica Fields and Celeste Hirschman "Citizenship Lessons in Abstinence-Only Sexuality Education," *American Journal of Sexuality Education*, vol. 2, no. 2, 2007.

Free Inquiry "Abstinence-Only Education Flunks," June/July 2008.

Kim Gandy "Abstinence-Only Education Just Says No to the Truth," *National NOW Times*, Spring 2008.

Jennifer L. Greenblatt "'If You Don't Aim To Please, Don't Dress To Tease' And Other Public School Sex Education Lessons Subsidized By You, the Federal Taxpayer," *Texas Journal on Civil Liberties and Civil Rights*, vol. 14, no. 1, Fall 2008.

Gardiner Harris "Teenage Birth Rate Rises For First Time Since '91," *New York Times*, December 16, 2007.

William Henderson "Away from Abstinence," *Advocate*, December 5, 2006.

Herizons "Abstinence Causes Pregnancy," Summer 2008.

Sharon Jayson "Today's Topic: Sex Education," *USA Today*, September 28, 2008.

Abigail Jones and Marissa Miley "Abstinence Approach Not the Only Sex-Ed Option," *USA Today*, October 31, 2007.

Leslie M. Kantor "Abstinence-only Education Violating Students' Rights to Health Information," *Human Rights: Journal of the Section of Individual Rights and Responsibilities*, vol. 35, no. 3, Summer 2008.

Deborah Kotz "A Debate About Teaching Abstinence," *U.S. News and World Report*, December 31, 2007.

Ruth Marcus "And Then There Were Fewer Than 30," *Contemporary Sexuality*, vol. 42, no. 10, October 2008.

Zach Miners "Debating Sex Ed," *District Administration*, June 2008.

Mother Jones "Virginity For Sale," November/December 2006.

Nation "Sexual Side Effects," December 3, 2007.

Nation's Health "Federally Requested Report Finds Abstinence Education Not Effective," June/July 2007.

Maryjo M. Oster "Saying One Thing and Doing Another: The Paradox of Best Practices and Sex Education," *American Journal of Sexuality Education*, vol. 3, no. 2, 2008.

Katha Pollitt "The People's Choice," *Nation*, December 8, 2008.

Anna Quindlen "Let's Talk About Sex," *Newsweek*, March 16, 2009.

Jordan Smith "Where Do CPCs Get Funding?" *Ms.*, Fall 2008.

Kate Stables "The Joy of Sex Education," *Sight and Sound*, May 2009.

M. J. Stephey "A Brief History Of: Abstinence," *Time*, March 2, 2009.

Amy Sullivan "How to End the War Over Sex Ed,"
Time, April 6, 2009.

Ray Tarleton "Squirm as You Learn," *Times
Educational Supplement*, April 17,
2009.

Jeff A. Taylor "Balance Sheet," *Reason*, January
2007.

USA Today "In Sex Ed, Abstinence-Only Loses
Support but Keeps Funds," December
26, 2007.

*Wall Street
Journal* "U.S. Teen Birth Rate Rises,"
December 26, 2007.

Alex Wayne "Hold That Abstinence," *CQ Weekly*,
March 2, 2009.

Barbara Dafoe
Whitehead "And Baby Makes Two,"
Commonweal, October 10, 2008.

Index

A

Abortions
    abstinence prevention
      method, 54, 77
    future pregnancies and, 80
    information inaccuracies, 29
    same-sex relationships and,
      92, 96
    STDs and, 29
    teen pregnancy and, 47
    U.S. data, 12, 13, 28
Abstinence
    advantages of, 27, 36–37,
      54–55
    avoidance of STDs, 7, 27
    definition, 36, 38
    individuals and, 84–87
Abstinence Clearinghouse, 78, 79
Abstinence-only education
    ACLU opposition to, 24–32
    Case Western University study,
      29
    censorship of information,
      27–28
    church and state separation,
      30–32
    comprehensive sex education
      vs., 45–47, 91–98, 99–101
    Congressional funding for, 24
    effectiveness of, 46, 53–54
    gay youth harmed by, 29–30
    health endangerment from,
      28–29
    ineffectiveness of, 26–27
    Obama's funding cuts for, 9
    parental support for, 41

    pregnancy prevention failure,
      83–90
    pregnancy prevention success,
      77–82
    Rector on, 11
    SPRANS program curricula,
      28–29
    successful programs, 55–56
    teen sex delayed from, 45–56
    teen sex not delayed from,
      57–67
    U.S. data, 24–25
    as violation of student's
      rights, 24–32
    See also names of individual
      programs
Abstinence-only education, spe-
  cific programs, 58–67
    behavioral impact, 61–62
    evaluation design, 60–61
    future considerations, 65–67
    knowledge of associated risks,
      62–63
    pregnancy perceptions/STD
      prevention, 64–65
    See also Families United to
      Prevent Teen Pregnancy; My
      Choice, My Future!; Recap-
      turing the Vision; Teens in
      Control
Abstinence plus education. *See*
  comprehensive sex education
The Abstinence Teacher (Perotta),
  12
ACLU (American Civil Liberties
  Union), 8, 24–32
ACLU v. Leavitt (2005), 31

Y

Z